THE ART OF BUYING & SELLING AT
FLEA MARKETS

BY BARRY BERG

Published by Hobby House Press, Inc.
Grantsville, Maryland
www.hobbyhouse.com

Acknowledgments

I want to thank my many thoughtful friends, relatives, customers and fellow dealers, who, often without knowing it, contributed to this book—a few I must mention by name.

John F. Matthews, of Brandeis University, inspired me when I was first becoming a writer, and taught me the importance of dramatic narrative and structure.

My sister, Diane Reeves, sparked my interest in collectibles; with her husband Bill they remain my close collaborators.

Marc Kessler has been a generous counselor, providing insight into the psychology of people and their passions for collecting.

Cal Hennig has been my personal aestheticist, teaching me to see what I am looking at.

Brigitta Boveland has guided me to look below the surface of objects and environments, and gives depth to my often superficial views.

Al Zuckerman has been my literary agent for more than three decades. I am grateful for his faith in me, and for founding Writers House which has become a second home.

Susan B. Cohen reads and comments on every line I write. She does this not because she is a literary agent and my wife, but because she says she actually likes my work. I don't question her too deeply on this.

Additional copies of this book may be purchased at $19.95 (plus postage and handling) from
Hobby House Press, Inc.
1 Corporate Drive, Grantsville, MD 21536
1-800-554-1447
www.hobbyhouse.com
or from your favorite bookstore or dealer.

Printed in the United States of America

ISBN: 0-87588-656-6

Table of Contents

Preface

Who is this book for? This book might interest you if:

- you are touched by the fact that old objects were used by people long gone, and you wonder what those people were like.

- you are intrigued by the form and function of things, and curious about how design and materials have changed.

- you have any interest in history

- you are amazed to learn that an Andy Warhol cookie jar sold for ten thousand dollars, and wonder who was dumb enough to pay ten grand for a cookie jar

- you then wonder, do I have a sellable cookie jar? And if so how can I find that buyer?

- you believe that an afternoon wasted by aimless browsing in a flea market is not wasted at all, and that one man's trash might indeed be another's treasure.

- it is your considered opinion that it might be no less wise to invest in Pez® dispensers as the stock market

- you want to decorate your apartment cheaply and nicely

- you have a curiosity about the unsettled weather that arises when psychology and economics interact, or

- you only want to become a more savvy shopper

This little Greek or Roman vessel is the oldest item I own, going back about 2000 years. I paid over $300 for it because I liked it. It was old, it was beautiful, it was in perfect condition. I may have overpaid, I don't know. This is not my area of expertise. But if I did overpay, I don't mind. I love it. Sometimes dealers should follow their hearts, like every other collector does.

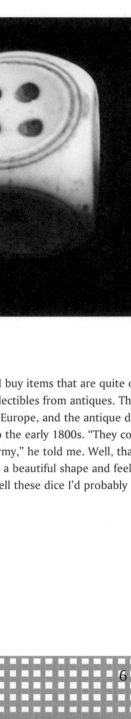

Occasionally I buy items that are quite old, and come close to the line that separates collectibles from antiques. The pair of dice are bone. They were purchased in Europe, and the antique dealer who sold them to me said they dated back to the early 1800s. "They could have been used by soldiers in Napoleon's army," he told me. Well, that may or may not be so, but they are old, and have a beautiful shape and feel. Gambling items are popular, and if I wanted to sell these dice I'd probably ask between $100 and $200 for them.

Eyecups were once common in medicine cabinets; people used them to wash out irritants in the eye. Today, young folk who lubricate their eyes with squirts from little plastic containers have no idea what these glass beauties are. While common eyecups sell for $5 to $25, the one pictured here has an uncommon shape, and would sell for around $75.

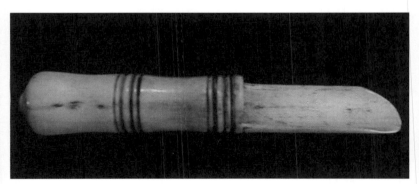

This bone item is an apple corer. It is English, and also dates to the early 1800s. There is novelty here, particularly for the collector of kitchen memorabilia, and I think it should go for $60 or so.

The items pictured above and right have enormous appeal to me because they were objects of every day life, used for the trivial tasks of opening bottles, clipping pages together, and holding papers down. Yet look at the artistry. Their condition and aesthetic, (together with the novel subject matter and design of the paperweight), make them rare and desirable. I would put at least $100 on the Harvard bottle opener, and three times that amount for the Hoffman paper clip and the John Eichleay, Jr. paperweight. I have included the underside of this paperweight to show its crimped glass backing. Only when the image is totally encased in glass can you be sure that it is original, and not some recent construction.

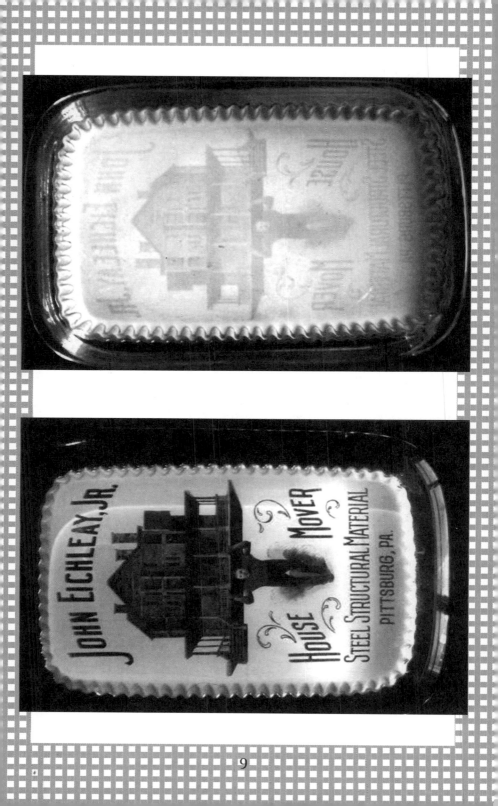

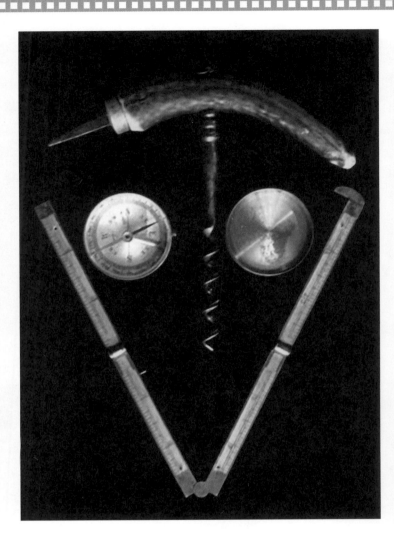

In a similar vein, the three tools pictured above, (a corkscrew, a compass, and a folding ruler), are collected today both for their use and their aesthetic value. If you need a corkscrew in the house, why not have a beautiful one that will not break? If you need a ruler, why not the novelty of a folding one that will fit in your pocket? The corkscrew and folding ruler should sell for $50 each, the small brass compass might be $15 less.

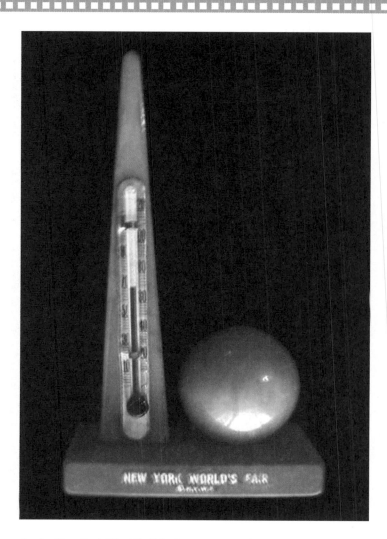

In the New York World's Fair thermometer, above, we again see value achieved by a combination of history, (World's Fairs are historic events), use, (it is a working thermometer), and aesthetic. In this case, however, there is added value because it is made of bakelite, an early form of plastic. Bakelite items are collected by thousands of people, so much so that the plastic itself may be thought of as having an intrinsic value, not so much as gold but probably more than silver. I have seen this little 1939 World's Fair thermometer being offered by vendors at prices up to $100, depending upon condition.

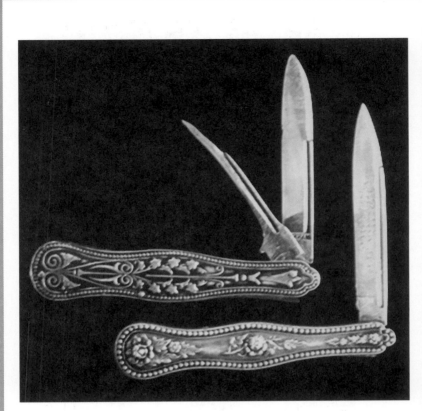

Above are a pair of American fruit knives. Fruit knives were popular status items with gentlemen of the 19th and early 20th Centuries. They were used at the dinner table, or on a picnic, to cut open a pear or an apple at meal's end. The blades were usually silver, since silver was thought best for cutting fruit (and not strong enough to cut much else), and the handles of these two are silver-plate. You can see that one even has a pick-blade, used for prying out seeds. There is some intrinsic value in these knives, a little use value (if one is careful), novelty value coming out of their particular use, and much aesthetic value in the decorations on the handles and the blades. These two are not particularly expensive examples of fruit knives, but they would still bring $50 to $70 each.

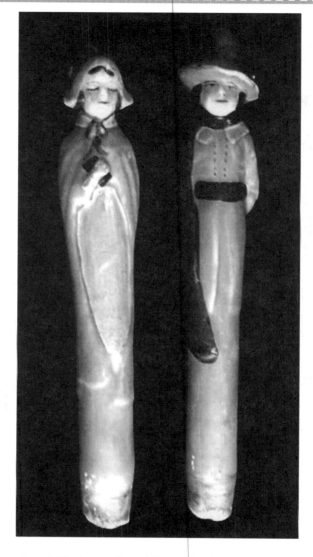

These figural Pilgrim candles are interesting because of the story
that came with them. Apparently, they were made as tourist items,
and sold in the Boston area in the 1930s and 1940s. Usually items
made for the tourist trade do not become collectibles. Collectors
prefer things that are true artifacts of a time and place. But, when
tourist items are made with great care and artistry, they transcend
their origin and can have enduring value. I would think this pair of
candles should sell for no less than $75.

This small figural pencil sharpener was produced to advertise Baker's Chocolate. Again we see the work and attention to detail that went into producing everyday objects – this little beauty was probably hand painted! In better condition she would command $75. With the paint chips, $45 is a more realistic selling price.

Introduction

This book is not about fine antiques. I think Chippendale chairs and Tiffany lamps are beautiful, but items that might be found in a museum and cost a year's salary live in a world apart from mine. Let me confess at the outset: Antiques are too elegant for my taste. I love caviar, and I will eat it happily twice a year, but I come from working class people who lived through the Depression; our heritage was potatoes and brown bread. Furniture had to be practical and withstand the assaults of many children. Lamps had to give light, and frankly paying the electric bill took precedence over contemplating styles of art; nouveau and deco were not in my early vocabulary. Also, I love the idea of discovering treasure, and it is most unusual to discover anything in the halls of Sotheby's and Christie's; their merchandise screams its value. But buying a Pez® dispenser for $15 and then finding a collector who is delighted to own it for $500? Purchasing a bag of marbles for $12 and selling them individually for $600? Buying a collection of advertising trade cards from a dealer in California for under a thousand and seeing that collection climb tenfold in value? Now *that* interests me. In short, although I love looking at objects in museums, I am most interested when I can touch and buy, and I can not afford items that cost $1000 and more. So this book is about objects that I can afford—interesting old stuff that costs $5, $10, $20. At over $50 I think twice. At over $100 it has to be special, and as a dealer I need to be fairly certain I can sell it quickly and for a profit.

Also, as a writer I have an historical interest in everyday life – how folks went about their chores and their businesses, and how they pursued their pleasures. So, as I became drawn into this world of "old stuff," I did not become an antique dealer, but rather a buyer and seller of *collectibles*, which we all own whether we know it or not. Grandpa's straight razor, now used for cutting string. The doorstop that came with the house. That photo album from the old country. Grandma's eyeglasses. Worthless stock certificates. Postcards and old magazines. Eyewash cups. Tin cans. Political campaign buttons. Corkscrews and bottle openers. Salt and sugar shakers. Expired credit cards. The pile of whiskey bottles sitting behind the shed. That condom tin in the back of the medicine cabinet. The list is endless. (Note: It is collect*ibles*, not collect*ables*. A plain rock is collect*able*; you can collect it if you wish. But no one wishes to. So it is not a collect*ible*.)

These artifacts of another day are found in cellars and attics and barns, in the backs of dresser drawers, buried in outhouses and sitting on shelves of country antique shops, and most interestingly and inexpensively, at that Sunday junk fair called the Flea Market.

The Flea Market

It is the most democratic institution around. A man wants to sell something, he pays a small fee for a space in an outdoor parking lot or a farmer's field, brings his own table, puts out his wares, and he's in business. He has no boss. His hours are his own. The government will ask him to report what he has made, but there is little oversight; this is frontier capitalism. Also, there is no middleman. Only a seller, an object offered, and a potential buyer who wanders by and stops at the table. He may pick up an item that strikes his eye and examine it. There is usually some small conversation over price, and the sale is made – or not. It is pure, and, in this hi-tech high-pressure media-crazed and highly regulated world of finance and business, its simplicity is elegant. Note: There are flea markets and there are flea markets. Since the sign has some cachet these days, any group of vendors selling bungee cords and t-shirts in an outdoor space can call themselves a flea market. I am talking about a market of vendors who sell old stuff culled from attics and garages and estate sales, from thrift shops, basements, yard sales and barns. Stuff that is nice, but useless. Stuff that no one wants anymore—no one but collectors.

Nevertheless, for many, the thought of buying at a flea market is intimidating. It was for me at the start. I didn't know the rules. I had no idea what the carved ivory chess set I was looking at should cost. I didn't know if it was old or if it was made yesterday. In many cases, there weren't even prices affixed to the items for sale. It was me against the vendor, and I didn't like the odds.

Let us not be naïve. At the outset the odds are not with you. You don't know anything, you have no basis from which to choose; there are unscrupulous people in the world, and the business of antiques and collectibles has its share. However, while there is some truth to the notion that the savvy and sometimes unethical vendor takes advantage of an unwary public, I am proud to report that the vast majority of vendors respect their customers and treat them fairly. And I am delighted to report that for every dealer who takes advantage of an ignorant customer, there are two knowledgeable collectors who will approach that dealer's table, spot an item within their own areas of expertise, and eat his lunch.

In the world of buying and selling at flea markets, it isn't the bigger fish that eat the smaller ones. It is the learned fish who eat the ignorant ones. I find it a not unpleasant thought that in this business you get paid for what you know.

And the leveling fact is that no one can know everything. Many vendors know surprisingly little, and this includes the items on their tables. Even if you are a flea market virgin, in a few months you can become knowledgeable in one or two areas and more than hold your own. So don't be intimidated.

A word on vendors:

This is a family joke: Two old tailors are sitting on their benches by the window, working with needle and thread in the fading afternoon light. One looks up and thinks for a moment. "You know," he says, "if I had Rockefeller's money I'd be richer than Rockefeller." "How's that?" replies the other. The first tailor returns to his stitching. "I'd take in a little sewing on the side."

Understand that vendors are strange folk. While many are our retired grandparents acquiring a tan while earning a second income, a fair number are a maladjusted lot, (perhaps, today, I should say an "otherly-adjusted lot," especially since I am one of them), who don't fit normal work. A few have chips on their shoulders; they like to think their buying and selling experience makes them superior. But as in other areas of life, self-deceiving narcissists are most vulnerable. A few years ago I shopped the Columbus Avenue flea market in New York City and a canny and experienced vendor tried to sell me an old toy tractor, in working order. He was asking $400. I thought it was a great looking piece, but I wasn't about to plunk down "four bucks" for an item in a category (toys) which I knew nothing about. I had no idea what a fair retail price for that tractor might be. So I replied to this dealer that the tractor was indeed very nice, and I moved on. Well, I see this vendor again a couple of months later, and our earlier exchange must have stuck in his mind because the minute he lays eyes on me, his cheeks bulge and his lip quivers.

"Do you know what you did?" he scolds. "Do you know what you passed up?" I hardly remembered our previous conversation, but he's red-faced now and chortling at me like I was the fool of the century. "That tractor?" he reminds me. "Someone bought it, ran it through an auction, and it sold for eight thousand dollars!" I still remember the contemptuous look on his face. At me. For *my* being such a dolt!

You see, amongst us dealers who do not specialize, but sell general collectibles, the truthful and self-reflective ones will admit that half the time we don't know what we're doing. We buy a thingmajig for $10, we try to sell it for $25, we're happy when we get $20. The fact that it's a green thingmajig is meaningless to us. We don't know that thingmajigs nearly always appear in blue and that knowledgeable collectors will pay several hundred dollars for a green one.

So don't be intimidated. Instead, learn. Walk the markets. Look and listen. Most importantly, ask questions.

The suspicious and paranoid vendor will think you are picking his brain and zealously guard the few bits of knowledge by which he makes his ignominious living. Ignore him. The smart vendor is pleased to share information and wants you as a long-term customer. He will explain fully and cheerfully. Ask what the object is, what its use was, why he has priced it the way he has. Personally, I am most respectful of polite ignorance, whether exhibited by myself or by another. I do, however, exercise common sense when I am the ignorant one, and I do not tie up another vendor's time with naive questions when he is busy with other customers.

Getting Started: Choosing A Category

There is too much to look at in a Flea Market. If you want to become a collector or a dealer you must discard whole categories, and limit yourself to a few. Find one or two which interest you, and in doing this, listen not to your head, but to your heart. That is, do not try to reason why that category entices, and never pick one because it is hot, for which you think, "if I learn all about baseball cards I can buy and sell them and make a killing." Once you, as a lay person, have become aware that a certain category of collectibles is "hot," that category is on the verge of meltdown; it is far too late to buy for short-term gain. But perhaps you once made pottery and find ceramics compelling. Or you happen to love the workmanship in old glass. Or you enjoy the gleam and romance of silver. Or are amazed at vintage watches, or carpenter's tools, or mesh purses, or the amount of detail, design, and sheer exuberant color that went into the lithography transferred onto an old tin can. Trust yourself. If at this moment you are unsure of what you like, walk around for a month and actively look. Passion will probably bloom.

So you've walked the markets, asked questions, homed in on a category or two, perhaps bought a book explaining the items and current prices within that category. Now that you've learned the dimensions of the pool, where it is shallow and where it is deep, it's time to dive in.

The Art of Buying

Your First Purchases

Buy the more common items in your category first. They will be less expensive. But buy them in fine to mint condition. If you buy an item in poor condition—rusted, badly scratched, chipped, torn, incomplete—understand that it will have no retail or trading value whatsoever. Conversely, a mint condition common item can often be bought at a surprising discount, precisely because it is common and the dealer knows he can find another. Understand that in this business it is often the case that what is easily found today will be scarce in a few years. Be aware, too, that warehouse finds regularly occur. One item within a category can suddenly become so common that everyone devalues it and the price drops dramatically. In 1990, a certain marbleized glass eye cup appeared on a dozen dealer tables at Brimfield. (Eye cups, eyewash cups, or eye baths are no longer in fashion; but decades ago they sat in our medicine cabinets and were used to wash the eye if an irritant got in.) It was a warehouse find, thousands had come out of the basement of an old drug store, every-one had them, and they were being sold at $8, $6, $4 each. I bought some at all those prices, finally stocking up at the lower levels. Over the next year or two I sold them slowly at $12 to $15 each. By 1995, when I had none left, the few dealers who still had stock were offering them at $45 each. The next year a pocket tobacco tin can called Red Jacket began showing up everywhere. It had a great graphic—a man in a red jacket riding a horse, beautiful color—and every one of them was in the same pristine condition. After satisfying myself that this wasn't a batch of reproductions, I bought one for $30, then saw a number at $20. I was sufficiently disheartened by the commonness of this tin can that I didn't buy more. At some later time, I sold the one I bought for $50, and today, if you can find them, Red Jacket tobacco tins are selling north of $80. The moral? If you know your category, and you suddenly see one item within it dirt cheap, and you're confident it isn't a reproduction, take the long view. Screw your courage to a sticking place and stock up. As a dealer you will make a handsome profit, as a collector you will have some wonderful duplicates to trade.

The Negotiation

It is a cool, sunny Sunday and you are in the market. You have ample money in your pocket including small bills – it is both smart and courteous for vendor and buyer to have plenty of tens and fives and ones so there is no problem with the purchase or with making change. You have your eyeglasses and a loop or small magnifying glass in your pocket. Remember, you are not in a store where the culture does not permit negotiation, and where you are dealing with a salesperson who has no authority to change price. This is a flea market; you are always dealing with the owner who has absolute authority over price. For many people the joy of this experience is the negotiation. So how to do it?

This is an important and nuanced skill, but one, which I think, is easily mastered. You will find a dealer, now and then, who will not negotiate – they have been through the hurly-burly of bickering and their prices are firm. Take these fine folk at their word. Decide if you want to pay their price for the item; then take it or leave it. But this rational stance is rare. Nearly all dealers expect you to negotiate. For goodness sake, they price their items to allow for your discount. Don't disappoint them.

There are two ways to proceed: You can ask the vendor if he can reduce the price, or you can make the first offer.

In the first instance, a good opening gambit is, "What are you asking for this?" This can be asked whether or not you see a price tag on the item. Because, phrased in this manner, you are noting that the tag price is just an *asking* price and not necessarily the lowest price the dealer will accept. This immediately opens the door to a negotiation. After the dealer announces the price, or directs your attention to the price tag, you can follow up with, "Can you do better on it?" (Note: Please do not say you are a dealer if you are not. It won't impress the vendor, who has heard this too many times to care. And all lies are a decrement; they chip away at your character until, finally, integrity is gone. Also, you may be asked for your tax number at the close of the sale.) The dealer will then probably quote a number 10%-20% below the tag price. At this point you are close to the line of take it or leave it. If you are a collector who is trying to build a relationship with this dealer, you will not come back with a lower counter offer. You will either accept that price or regretfully walk away. If you want to be hard, and not endear yourself to that dealer for future consideration, you can come back with your own figure, say 10% lower than his discount, claiming ever so politely that this is really what you had in mind, and all you can afford. If the dealer offers you a full 20% off, do not try to reduce it an additional 20%. It won't fly and will only offend. (Note again: It is generally the new and unsophisti-cated collector who is the stiffest haggler. The knowledgeable collector knows market values, knows the dealer has to make a profit, and is more interested in forming an alliance, so the dealer will call him with new finds, than in saving a couple of bucks.)

If you decide to go the other route, and offer a price first, obey two courtesies. Make the offer reasonable, 20% to 30% off is within bounds – anything greater than 30% will likely offend. And be prepared to purchase the item, on the spot, with cash or a good check, (*not* a credit card), if the dealer accepts.

The reasons for these courtesies follow common sense. If I am a dealer with a tag price of $50 on an item, and you offer $25, you are in effect saying you think $25 is a reasonable selling price. If that is so, you are implying that either I do not know the value of my merchandise (otherwise how could I ask twice retail value) or I do know and I am gouging. In either case, I will be offended. If I am truly gouging, I am not a vendor with whom you want to do business. And if I am ignorant of my merchandise, you may want to take advantage of me when my price is too low, but it does you no good to expose me when my price is too high.

It should go without saying, but keep your cool. Dealers are like everyone else; some are reasonable and some are nuts. It does no good to react emotionally to difficult personalities. I constantly see vendors who have outlandishly high prices on items in categories I know very well. I do not take it as my job to educate them. Instead, I either walk away from their tables or I look through their wares to see if in their ignorance they have created a bargain for me. For example, a vendor has a collection of advertising trade cards, which he has been selling slowly but steadily for $3 a piece. This year he learns that trade cards are hot and are bringing good money. But he doesn't know the valuable ones, so he erases the $3 and he pencils in a new price of $20 each. Why $20? Why not? It is outrageous, but this dealer has decided he doesn't want to get ripped off, and this is his way of protecting himself. It is poor protection. Now the casual collector will not buy any of his cards because they are too expensive. And the knowledgeable collector, or dealer, will look through the lot only because some advertising trade cards sell for $200. As a dealer or as a collector, there is no substitute for doing your homework.

The second courtesy likewise follows common sense. If at any time you make an offer on an item, either as an opening offer or as a counter-offer to the vendor's discount, you are ethically bound to buy the item at that price. You may not make an offer, have the vendor accept it, and then say, "Let me think about it," and walk away. That sort of fishing expedition, to determine an acceptable price without following through, is exploitative. Imagine the situation reversed, and the vendor did that to you. You see a camera you want marked $80. You ask nicely for a better price, and the vendor replies you can have it for $65. As he sees you go for your wallet he adds, "Actually, now that I know you're willing to pay $65, let's make it $70!"

Finally, it is excellent Karma and even good business to occasionally pay full sticker price. If I see something inexpensive, something I know I can make a profit on, I will often buy it at that price. It is much appreciated by the vendor, it raises you in his esteem, and it brings the transaction to a higher, nobler level. It makes everyone feel good, and isn't that worth a few dollars? (All right, I can hear the chorus of nays, more's the pity for us.) When a collector buys from me that way, you can be sure that I keep him in mind when I am shopping. And when I find something special I put it away, and wait until I can offer it to him, first.

I briefly mentioned that vendors need to make a profit on the items they sell. Let me amend this obvious fact to say that vendors, for their hard work and time put in, deserve to make a profit on items they sell.

This, too, is common sense. However, when the public learns that vendors aim for a minimum markup of 100%, it raises a collective eyebrow and thinks, "I don't have to pay that. I don't even have to settle for a 20% discount. I can buy my treasures from the original seller at half the price."

Yes, dear reader, you can. You can spend hundreds of hours scouring antique shops, shows, and flea markets, looking for that original seller. You can check every yard sale and estate sale you see advertised in the newspaper. You can make trips to Brimfield on the east coast, to the Rose Bowl on the west coast, and to all those wonderful market extravaganzas in between. You can spend full weekends looking, paying hotel and car costs along the way. You can do all that and still not be sure you're going to find even one item for which you are looking. Also, it takes only a little reflection to realize that a 100% markup is not a 100% profit. Say I buy a Chinese vase for $50. I take it to the flea market and put a sticker price of $100 on it. I bring this vase to the market 5 times, and finally someone likes it, and offers me $70. I reply I can take no less than $85, and we settle on $80. So now I've made $30 on a $50 investment. Not bad. But I have to pay rent for the space in which I am selling. And unless I have a big enough car to bring my own tables, I must rent the tables. I drive my wares to the market. Gas and tolls? Tax on the profit? Not to mention my time and comfort—waking up before dawn; loading and unloading my car; sitting and standing and shuffling for ten hours, and often sitting and standing and shuffling in blazing heat, freezing cold, and driving rain. I have not even mentioned the possibility that I will drop or chip the vase while packing or unpacking it, or that a gust of wind might knock it over. Now what does that 100% price tag markup turn out to be? I don't know. No dealer does. No dealer really wants to.

Etiquette and Courtesies

As all environments do, the Flea Market has its own rules of behavior.

Possession is all ten points of the law. If you have an object in your hand, and you are contemplating buying it, it is yours alone to consider at that moment. By holding it in your hand you have obtained an option to buy. But when you put it down, you relinquish that right. If someone else picks it up they now have that option, and you may not go to the dealer and say, "See that fountain pen that guy is holding? I want to buy it!" My sister, Diane, who used to go to estate sales in California, tells of couples entering, together with a rush of others, running to a table, and literally spreading their arms wide over everything on that table, staking their claim so no one else can even look until they finish. If you've picked up an item that you like, don't put it down until you have decided you don't want it, or until you are negotiating with the dealer for it.

Many dealers keep their best items in closed cases with glass tops. Please do not open a case uninvited. Asking if you can open a case to look is more than just a courtesy. Dealers can be skittish about shoplifting, and by bringing yourself to the attention of the dealer you are providing a needed reassurance that you are not thinking of pocketing his gold cigar cutter and walking away.

A word on shoplifting. My friend Ike has a sign at his table. "Shoplifting is an illness. Don't get sick here." Many dealers are paranoid about shoplifting. I am not. But I don't sell gold jewelry. My items are relatively inexpensive collectibles, and since I have a hard enough time selling them, I can't imagine that some thief who wants fast cash, and pockets one of my paperweights, will do very well in a pawn shop. No, anyone who shoplifts from me will be either a kleptomaniac or a collector or dealer who wants the item very badly, but doesn't want to pay the price. Those are both sicknesses, and rare. From time to time, I discover I have lost track of some merchandise. Part of the time, I'm sure I sold the piece and never wrote it down. More often I probably just lost it, particularly if it was a small item like a pinback button that fell out of a case. Occasionally, it turns up a year later in a box I forgot I had. And yes, occasionally someone will have pocketed it. Only once did I catch the felon in the act. He was an older guy, with a stubble beard. A little disheveled. Not well dressed. It was late fall, and as I was sitting in my chair, watching, my jaw dropped as I saw him slip something – perhaps an ashtray, in any event an item of slight worth – into his coat pocket. I leaped up, full of outrage.

"What are you doing?"

Startled, he turned and faced me. "What are you doing?" I demanded. "Take that out of your pocket!"

Sheepishly, he did so, and put the thing back on the table. This all happened in seconds, without thought. I didn't call flea market security. I didn't yell for the police. Instead, I began to scold him as though he were an 8-year-old boy who had taken a cookie.

"What's your name?" I began. I could hardly hear his answer; his eyes were on the ground. "Bill," he muttered. "Bill, you should be ashamed of yourself!" And I went on for several minutes in that vein. He apologized. I huffed and puffed. He said he didn't realize what he was doing. Finally, I ordered him to leave the market. "I don't ever want to see you doing that again!" I told him. It was preposterous. I was sending him to his room!

He left and I breathed deeply. I was hurt by this man. Not financially. Even if he had gotten away with the thing, it would scarcely have mattered. But he had done something hurtful to me and shameful to himself, and I wanted him to know that. It never crossed my mind that he was a danger to society, and that I should call the police. (Clearly I have my own character flaws.) I didn't think of him as a criminal. He was a squirrelly old man. But the thought that he could do this to me! How dare he!

I never saw Shoplifter Bill again.

But stories that illustrate the reverse, abound. Often a customer will point out an item that has fallen off my table. Customers regularly go through my cases, (with and without my permission!), and I can't always watch. The people who buy and sell collectibles are honorable – there is no getting around it. When I am buying at Brimfield, it always happens that I go up to a table, find an item I want, and there is no vendor in sight to take my money. I get annoyed and sometimes angry. I want to buy the thing, and I can't. The thought never crosses my mind to put the item in my pocket and walk off, muttering, (read "rationalizing"), "serves him right." And apparently it doesn't cross other people's minds either because if it did, you wouldn't see so many vendors cavalierly walk off and leave their booths unattended. Prudence is always recommended, and I watch my wares as much as the next fellow does. But I don't think I will be shoplifted, I treat people as though they are honest, and so far it has worked out just fine.

But back to Etiquette and Courtesies.

If you are interested in an object, it is fine to ask the vendor about it. This is how you learn, and sellers should be willing to tell you about their treasures. But please, *please* do not start to tell the dealer the story of how you had hundreds of baseball cards or comic books as a child, and how your mother threw them away. Truly, and please take my word for this, no one cares about what you once had. Also, the vendor is working. I know it's the weekend. I know he may not look like he's working, sitting in his chair, trying to eat his egg salad sandwich without getting any on his shirt, looking for a flat surface for his coffee. But his eyes are watching his merchandise, and his job is not to reminisce with you about your childhood but to down his lunch and get up to service people who are really interested in buying his stuff. Imagine if on Monday, (his day off), he walked into your office, found you at your desk, and full of wistful bonhomie began, "You know I had an office job once. It was back in '85 and it was with this insurance company …"

And speaking of egg salad sandwiches, the vendor's space is not public property where you can spread out on the grass beside his table and have a picnic. If you are carrying a drink in your hand, please don't set it down on his table. If you smoke, it is discourteous to discard wrappers or butts in the dealer's area.

There is a difference between examining an object and playing with it. Don't wind a spring; let the owner do it for you. If you are interested in a cigarette lighter, it is fine to thumb the wheel once to see if you get a spark. It is not fine to do it ten times, or show your buddy the cool way you used to slap your Zippo® against your leg to get it opened and lit. You can pick up a Buck Rogers Space Gun, but please don't relive your childhood by pulling the trigger half a dozen times. Moving parts will wear down and break, and if that happens while you are enjoying yourself there will be a tense moment between you and the dealer. Some will insist, "you broke it, you bought it." Others will ask for some lesser amount, to cover their purchase cost. A few will absorb the loss themselves. I suppose we have all had mishaps. In a shop I once turned a bottle upside down to check the bottom, and a stopper, which I hadn't secured in my hand, fell off and chipped on the floor. The owner immediately tried to make me feel better, and told me not to worry about it. I was so grateful that I bought something else I only marginally wanted, and I have instituted that sort of "no-fault" policy myself.

Now that you've begun to buy, perhaps even started a collection, you might be feeling cocky. A little knowledge is a dangerous thing, Swift says. Be prudent. You will make mistakes; you have to. You will act precipitously. You will buy something without examining it carefully, and later notice the critical defect. Half the time you will feel the flush of a great purchase at a great price; the other half you will drown in buyer's remorse. Another rule: Unless an item has been misrepresented by the vendor, or unless the vendor has a policy of return, (and few do), do not try to take it back. There is a code of ethics in frontier capitalism. No one is forcing you to buy anything. No one is hurrying you, and no one should be hiding anything from you. You have all the time you want to examine the object, and ask questions about it. If in the end you make a mistake, and you will, live with it. Consider it part of your tuition.

A word on children. Sane advice would be to not take children to flea markets. They want to touch *everything*. But if you are brave, and if you are not committed to serious shopping yourself, I would take the other view. I think the flea market is a wonderful and educational place for children. They will learn that they can't touch every-thing, but, if they have asked permission first, (and what a nice lesson that is), they may touch some things. They can open and close a folding ruler that their great-grandfather might have owned. They can hold a compass and find north. They will observe a wind-up phonograph – there was music before CDs, even before electricity! They may see a typewriter for the first time! Of course vendors are nervous about children, and, as a parent myself, I have learned to quickly determine the tolerance of each vendor for my son's natural behavior.

My Three Best Tips
on Buying

Buy from dealers who do *not* specialize in your category. One of the categories that I sell is corkscrews. When I walk through a large show, such as Brimfield, I come across two or three dealers who specialize in corkscrews and related wine collectibles. Their display is impressive, filled with old, beautiful, expensive items. I look at these displays carefully and note the values that these experts place on their inventory. They know this category better than I do, and I learn from them. But clearly I can not buy from these vendors. If they sell a certain double-lever French corkscrew to me for $95, how can I hope to get much more? But, when I travel on to a booth in the next aisle, and I see an older couple from rural Maine who don't seem to specialize in anything at all, but have odds and ends scattered on their tables that they found cleaning out houses and buying from pickers "Down-East," if they do have a corkscrew lying on a table, I have a chance of buying it at a good price. They don't know corkscrews. They don't much care about corkscrews. If they bought one for $2 they might sell it for $20 and feel they have done very well. And indeed they have. And I might buy that corkscrew and sell it for $60 because I am interested in corkscrews and do know what the better ones look like. When you don't specialize you can't know everything about your stuff. You make your money across the board, buying inexpensively and selling for a profit. As generalist dealers they made their money and they should wish me well making mine. As I wish well the specialist who has a deeper knowledge than I do, and who buys that same corkscrew from me for $60 because he knows he can get $125 for it, perhaps even having a customer in hand. There is room in this business for buying and selling on all levels, with many degrees of knowledge; the flea market is not only an exemplar of frontier capitalism, it is also a seat of grass-roots democracy. And as such, it showcases a fundamental democratic virtue: Industry and knowledge get paid, laziness and ignorance lose out.

But what if you walk by a flea market table, or for that matter a table at the celebrated Triple Pier Show in New York City, and you see an object that plucks the strings of every covetous fiber in your body? You want this object more than you want power or sex. What to do? Obviously, you don't want to show the depth of your lust. The dealer is as sensitive to the scent of your desire as any shark ever was to the smell of blood. Display it and your discount is gone. But it is poor strategy, as well as poor manners, to bad-mouth the piece. We must assume that the dealer knows his merchandise; he probably had the same smitten reaction when he bought it. It does not help your cause to examine it carefully, purse your lips, and utter, "Tsk, tsk, how lovely, but look at this spot of rust!" or "I'd be really interested, but isn't the paint flaked just a bit, here?" My second "Best Tip" is this: Denigration does not work. You wouldn't be talking about the thing if you weren't interested, and you are setting up an adversarial relationship with the dealer. It is far better to seek a collegial relationship between you; it is far better to flatter the dealer. Without letting the awful truth that you'd mortgage your first born for the thing show through, compliment the dealer on the beauty or rarity or charm of the piece. Join him in admiring it. The dealer will begin to like you, and consider you, as he considers himself, a person of discernment. With rue (and feigned resignation) in your voice, tell him it is only a question of price that stands between your mutual desires – his wanting to sell it and your wanting to buy it. Chances are excellent you will receive his best price. And if he doesn't come down, swallow your pride and pay the tab. Tomorrow you will have your find-of-the-year. The day after you won't remember the extra amount you paid.

Note: I am of two minds about walking away to think about an object I intensely desire, but which strikes me as too highly priced. My first mind tells me to try to forget it. If it stays with me, if the thing has already gotten under my skin, I can come back and buy it. But my other mind counters, (with experience to back up its claim), that when I walk away from an item I truly want, the gods will insure that another buyer immediately appears, and that my treasure will not be there when I return. Take your pick.

In the course of this essay, I mention a number of items I have bought cheaply and sold well – a bag of marbles and an early Pez® dispenser were noted at the beginning, and more will follow. These particularly interesting items came from outside this country. Different cultures place different values on their objects, and common "old stuff" in one country may be scarce and desirable in another. If you are lucky enough to be able to travel, my third "Best Tip" is to try to buy outside the country. I heartily recommend the flea markets of London, Paris, Brussels, Rotterdam, and especially any found in small European towns. Also helpful is the fact that in the last decade the dollar has been strong relative to European currencies, and is now hovering around par with the Euro. My friend Dorien, in Belgium, bought a beautiful photograph album with pictures of European royalty of the 19th Century. She paid a little over $100 for it. In a year or so I more than doubled that investment, and we both made out well. I have taught my friends Peter and Brigitta, who own a house in France, about vintage eye cups. Whenever they come across good ones, they buy them for me, usually for the equivalent of $10 to $15. I sell them here in the U.S, for $30 to $60. And my wife, Susan, has relatives in Montreal. When we go to Canada, I can sometimes buy quite well, even in shops, because as I write these words, the Canadian dollar is valued at two-thirds of the U.S. dollar.

But it is necessary to recognize that this international aspect of the collectibles business works both ways. Another vendor I know specializes in high quality costume jewelry. Once a year he flies to Italy, and travels the length of that country selling his jewelry to Italian dealers. This "reverse" business model has historical reasons. It seems that the Italians, particularly, have a long history of loving and buying expensive jewelry. But of course not everyone there can afford the precious gemstones, so a strong market in quality costume jewelry emerged. Much of this costume jewelry, also called paste, was produced in Europe, but America, (which was not devastated by two World Wars), has a history and a reputation for producing high quality costume jewelry. So many Italians want the American product. Once again it is astonishing to learn how politics, economics, even war play roles in the public's choice of what items are desired, and how they are priced.

Buying Collectibles As An Investment

If you have done your homework, putting together a considered collection is one of the best investments you can make. For starters, you are buying items that you thoroughly know. How many New York Stock Exchange companies can you research so completely? But it is faulty thinking to collect with that in mind. You cannot walk through a flea market and know, with any degree of certainty, what will increase in value over the next decades. Everyone says this, and it is true – the most valuable collections are the ones put together through love and commitment. If you buy what you love you will educate yourself, you will develop that discerning eye. *This* will lead to purchases that will increase in value. *This* will give you the courage to buy the most expensive items in your area of interest, and those are the buys, which, over time, will be the most profitable. If you buy only the items you find at a discount, you may be a good dealer but you will never be a great collector. The great collectors become experts in their field and will never hesitate to pay a market-breaking price for the truly unique item. (The point is, they know what is unique; they are getting premium value for premium price. And in my experience premium value always outstrips premium price).

Here is another story. A close friend bought a collection of political pinback buttons for $1000. There were about a thousand pieces in the collection; most were new, but about a dozen were quite old, and, my friend knew, were likely to be quite valuable. He paid cash for the collection and ran home. Quickly, he took out his price guides for political pinback buttons. (Ted Hake has written three such books; they are so complete, and the pictures so clear and detailed, that they have become bibles to everyone in the hobby.) The first pin he looked up was an Al Smith button. If it was genuine, it would be worth around $600. It was a worthless reproduction. The second was a Herbert Hoover. Worth $400. Except that this one was a reproduction as well. A Truman followed. Again, worthless. And down the line he went. Until he came to a Warren Harding pin that was scarcely a pin at all – although it had a large, crude fastener on the back. The thing was a metal cutout, covered with paper, and on the paper were pictures of Harding and his Vice-President. This one wasn't in the book. It was very weird. And in the Land of Collectibles, weird is good. My friend lived with hope.

He took that Harding pin to Brimfield the next year, and as luck had it he was visited by one of the biggest political pinback button collectors in the country. The collector asked, as he always did, "Have you got anything new?" My friend said, "I have something I've never seen before. Tell me what you think about it." And he went into his case and pulled out this strange Harding jugate. (A jugate is a repre-sentation of a President together with his Vice-President.) My friend had experience. He didn't look at the piece as he pulled it out, but kept his eyes on the collector's face. The collector didn't blink. He didn't show interest or boredom. He turned the thing over in his hand and said, "Well, I haven't seen it before either."

"You think it's genuine?" my friend asked.

"Looks it," the collector replied. "How much do you want for it."

The moment of truth. My friend swallowed. "I really don't know what to ask," he countered honestly. Political pinbacks can sell for any price from $1 - $25,000. "I should run it through an auction."

"Well, why don't you just throw out a figure you'd be happy with," the collector replied pleasantly. He was a bit more experienced than my friend.

"Fifteen hundred dollars," my friend replied.

"You'd be happy with that? I mean, that's an ok figure for you?"

My friend simply nodded. And the collector took out a small wallet and began filling in American Express checks of $100 each.

That is how a great collector buys. And how grand investments are created. Was the Harding piece worth $1500? My friend didn't know. The collector didn't know. It didn't really matter. He knew what he was doing. He knew the rare pieces and the common pieces, and it was worth $1500 to him.

I believe that having a passion and investing in that passion – and I mean investing time for study as well as investing money – can be one of life's joys. And at the end of the day you will have made a great investment. The problem with this course of action is that it is so hard to sell the things we love. Consider your collection part of your estate then. You will enjoy it for your life, and your heirs will benefit nicely after you are gone.

The Art of Selling

Most flea market vendors who sell more than once (the one or two time sellers are simply trying to dispose of the contents of their houses, and are not really in business) begin in one of two ways. Either they are collectors who decide that they want to sell off part of their collection. Or they begin with the idea that they would like to build a small business, and start as uncertain buyers, taking a chance that their purchases will lead to a profit.

The collectors have a clearer path. They know a category well; they know the dealers and their fellow collectors in that category. They have stock and they know how to price their wares. Their difficulty comes from the very specialization that provides the benefit. A collector of Roseville pottery decides to sell off half his collection. And since he is still a collector, he will very likely choose the lesser half, the items he bought early on when he didn't know what he was doing. So he picks 25 pieces, wraps them carefully, rents a space, and puts them out. The problem is this. Of the thousand people who pass by his table that day, how many of them will be Roseville collectors? How many will be interested in buying a piece of pottery of any make? His day will be long and boring. And when a Roseville collector does stop at his table, he likely won't want our new vendor's "mistakes." He will want the choice pieces, too. It will be hard for our specialist vendor to make many sales, and eventually he may find that the general flea market population will not support him. He may need to sell at a show that emphasizes good pottery. And he will have to pay a much higher rent to sell in this specialized market.

The beginning generalist vendor has a different problem. What to buy, and at what price? My advice here is the same as I offered above. Go with your heart. Find stuff that speaks to you. If you love it, someone else will, too. But unlike the new collector, you are buying for resale, so although you must follow your heart, you may not ignore your brain. You have to buy low and sell high. Or buy high and sell higher. And the difference must be worth your time and effort.

There is no way you can do it right the first time. It must be trial and error. One way to start is to become a "picker" (someone who does not set up a table himself, but rather looks to buy with the hope of selling to established vendors). You have been walking the markets. Presumably you have gotten to know some vendors, talked to them, become friendly. Find one who you like and who sells things that interest you, and try to shop for him. You will be selling to him dirt cheap; you won't make money on some items and you might even lose on a few. But you will have no overhead, either. You will work at your convenience. Your monetary risk will be small, and you will learn because your new vendor friend will teach you. If you can sell him items that he needs at wholesale prices, it will be in his self-interest to educate you.

Eventually, if you have the entrepreneurial spirit, you will want to do it for yourself. It is less intimidating than it sounds. The start up cost is negligible, so there isn't much to lose. You must go to your State authority and get a resale tax number. You need to keep records for tax purposes – what you've spent and what you've earned. You have to determine what it is you want to sell, and what prices to put on your wares. Then you only have to rent the space.

Note: There are several venues for selling. The easiest and probably least expensive is the yard or garage sale. But yard sales are mostly reserved for old clothes, ratty furniture, children's books and toys and the like. You could spend a week of Sundays before finding a good collectible at a yard sale, so most collectors and dealers do not frequent them. Also, a quarter is actually a unit of currency here. Bottom line—you are not going to get anything like fair value for your collectibles by running a yard or garage sale. Two levels up are the Antique and Collectible Shows. But here the entrance fees can be steep, and you need a couple of tables filled with good merchandise to make doing it worth while. For getting started, the right entry level really is your local flea market. Your neighbor to the left will be filling his tables with yard sale remainders; your neighbor to the right will be offering quality antique prints. You will fit in, whatever your bring. But still take care—you will probably have a choice of flea markets in your area. Follow two criteria in deciding which to choose. 1) Pick one that has a number of regular collectible dealers; this is the one to which buyers of collectibles will come. 2) choose a market with a modest set up fee. No use spending a bundle in this beginning period, when you will be making most of your mistakes.

The Set-Up

There are no rules about how to set up your space. Your own sense of organization and order, your own aesthetic tastes, will dictate. There are bridge tables with torn tops holding buckets of stuff, disorganized, dirty, and unpriced, and there are tables adorned with clean and pressed fire-retardant tablecloths, upon which beautiful collectibles are artfully arranged. And there is everything in between. Follow your instincts and you will find your niche, and learn something about your own natural sense of order and aesthetic in the bargain. You will need to decide if you want cases or not. How expensive is your merchandise, and how concerned are you about theft or damage? Common sense applies, but my own preference is to let the public handle my wares (not gold rings—I am egalitarian, but I am not stupid). I know that when I go to a table or into a shop and everything is in a case, I am much less inclined to buy. It is an inconvenience to get the owner to open it, and usually shows more of an interest than I might feel. Some vendors look for this – they only want serious buyers handling their merchandise. I enjoy having people touching my stuff. It promotes a friendly atmosphere, and, who knows, I might make a sale to a customer who didn't even know how much she wanted the thing until she had it in her hand.

I also think that, although disarray has a certain charm and some vendors make the case that the public wants to treasure hunt so you really should "bury" things for them, our fourth grade teachers were right and neatness counts. It is nice to approach a table where collectibles have been thoughtfully bought and laid out. All my bottles are together, next to my other glass items. All my nutcrackers are in one area, surrounded by like items such as bottle openers, letter openers, and corkscrews. When I bring paper or cardboard (and I generally don't to open air markets – rain, wind, and sun are no friends to paper) they have an area on a table all their own. Postcards, trade cards and even larger paper such as billheads and photographs go in 3-ring binders. My tin cans sit on a unit of rising shelves, to give them visibility and to save table space. And my pinback buttons are all arranged by category and set in glass cases, with folks invited to open the tops and check out any that might interest them.

Note: Don't confuse the customer. I have no data for this, but it is my conviction that too many choices can depress sales. There is a reason small birds fly in flocks. If a hawk sees a bird alone, it has little trouble swooping in for the kill. But with fifty or a hundred birds flying together, sweeping and swerving in unison, the predator has difficulty picking out any single bird. It begins to track one and then is disconcerted by another. The hesitation costs him, and all the birds of the flock get safely away. Don't put out a disconcerting number of things. Allow your customer to focus. Allow him the time to weigh the pros and cons of the purchase. If you see a potential buyer is conflicted, go over and genially ask if you can be of help. If the answer is no, go away and let him continue his inner debate. If yes, talk enthusiastically and knowledgeably about the item. Educating your customer is the best way to close the sale.

Bring a chair. Bring plastic coverings for your table, in case of a sudden shower. Also bring a beach umbrella and prepare to tie it to a table leg, to provide shade for both you and for your cases, particularly if you have items that can't stand a high temperature. In the hot weather glass cases become little hothouses, and you don't want to have a nice gold watch sitting under glass directly exposed to the August sun. As I mentioned above, printed colors on paper, cloth, or tin – particularly red – will fade in a direct sun.

Now, checking your list, make sure you have packed:
- an insulated jacket and thermal socks and shoes if it is cold

- an umbrella if it's rainy or hot
- enough food and drink to hold you for the day
- a companion to take over for you when you need to go to the bathroom
- a pocket full of small bills for change
- a bunch of bags for all the sales you will make, and
- some newspaper for wrapping

Now you are in business!

But before you dress and pack and try to sell your first item to your first customer, stop for a moment. Take a breath and evaluate your goal. Is this a one shot deal or do you think you'd like to do this regularly. If you really wish to sell everything you own that day you can come close to doing that by pricing your items ridiculously low. But if you want anything approaching market value for your wares, you will be making many trips to this flea market, paying many rents, standing in the heat and cold many times, waiting for the sales. It is easy to see the direct relationship between time and money – the lower the price, the faster the item will sell. This calculation is personal. For myself, over the years I have edged more and more to keeping prices reasonably low. There is always more stuff to buy, and cash flow is a good thing.

How Much to Sell For?
(And How Much to Pay?)

In answering the above questions you are, in effect, adopting a business model. Within your categories, you are placing yourself at the high end or at the low. I have a friend, Steve, who has a remarkable business model. He buys at country auctions, and looks for box-lots of low-grade stuff, which he gets cheap. Often, at the end of the auction, when almost no one is left, $20 will buy a box with 50 odd items – things the auctioneer did not think worthwhile to sell individually, or did not have the time to sell. Steve buys these lots and puts the items out on his table for $3 to $10 each. At the end of the day he might have made $200 on his $20 purchase. After a few exposures, Steve can now box the items that didn't sell and consign them back to the same auction where another dealer might pay $10 for the lot. It's neat, ecologically virtuous, and extremely labor intensive. Not for everyone, but it works for him. (Note: $20 seems to be a magic number these days. An object priced below $20 will sell as an impulse buy. After all, $15 today will barely buy you a Big-Mac and a movie with popcorn. At over $20, people feel they are spending money, and even though the value may be better, the wallet doesn't open as readily.)

Another vendor I know has a different business model. He buys at yard sales and also at low-end rural auctions, but only furniture, and for $20 or $30 he buys pieces that look awful and are in disrepair. He loads them in his pickup, repairs them, strips them, and refinishes them. Then he brings no more than ten of these attractive, fully-restored pieces of "country furniture" to his space and each dresser set or bookcase or table is priced at $200 or better. One sale more than covers his costs for the day.

My colleague Karl does business yet a different way. Karl specializes in watches, and the market for watches is more precise than most. Karl can look at a watch being offered at $150, and know he can sell it to another dealer quickly for $200. And if he waited for an interested retail customer, he could get $250. So Karl will buy that watch even without a discount. Now he can quickly turn it over for his $50 profit. Or he can wait, hoping to find his collector who will pay him the higher retail price.

There are other factors that control the price I might pay for an item. In this world of frontier capitalism I might have knowledge another dealer does not have, but I might also have a customer in hand. One of my nicest and most interesting clients is the granddaughter of Rube Goldberg. Rube is best known for the fabulous mechanical contraptions he drew as cartoons – you know, a mouse nibbling cheese, causing a weight to shift on a scale, which releases a ball down a chute that strikes a match which lights a candle that burns through a string … and on and on, until, in the end, the device causes a swizzle stick to stir your martini, without you having to get up from your chair. But Rube also designed comic pinback buttons, normally one-inch diameter cartoon pins, which were given away in the 1910s and 1920s as promotions for cigarette and gum companies. So as I browse flea markets and shops, I look for Rube Goldberg pins, and I have a guaranteed sale for each one with his name on it. If I go to an auction, and see a collection of comic pins for sale, I can usually outbid other dealers because I have a definite sale that they don't have. As in any other business, connections count.

There are as many business models as there are creative entrepreneurs. With interest, observation, and a little experience you will develop your own.

Telling A Story

I am a writer by trade; I *like* telling stories. It wasn't until I had been in this business for a few years that I realized I had not stopped telling stories when I started selling collectibles. Nor had I left behind my early passion for philosophy. Nor my later interest in psychology.

Let me explain.

By itself, the collectible or antique sitting on the table is a collection of molecules structured by human hands into an object of some practical or decorative use. Until it has *meaning* it is nothing. Meaning gives it value. And it has meaning because we place it in a context.

I used to live on an island off the coast of Maine. There was very little sand on the beaches of this island, but there were countless pebbles. Each morning I would walk up and down a small beach, after the tide went out, examining the pebbles. I would let my eyes drift over thousands of them, until, not every day but on some days, a particular pebble took my eye. It was not round and smooth like the others, but angular, with faceted surfaces, and definite edges only a little dulled by the pounding surf. I had found an arrowhead. A tribe of Indians had lived on that island hundreds of years before, and this was an artifact from that culture. At least I thought so. It sure looked like an arrowhead. No, I was sure of it. But someone could always argue that it was simply a pebble with a different shape. If it *was* an arrowhead, it had a context, a meaning, and a value. If it was just another pebble on the beach it was worthless.

But which was it?

It was neither, dear reader. It was nothing. It remains nothing unless I can tell a story (and when I say "story" I mean a story I believe is true, backed with evidence for that belief) and until someone believes that story. When someone believes my story, and the two of us are in agreement, I now have an arrowhead. If no one believes my story, I have nothing. (And yes, a tree falling in the middle of a forest, with no one to hear it, makes no sound.)

So philosophy, economics, and narrative meet. If I know the history (context) of the items on my table, and if I can tell a convincing story, I have a much better chance of selling them, and for a better price.

Good stories, with context, create excitement. A cookie jar may sell for $100. But if that cookie jar belonged to Andy Warhol – and what a great story that is – it becomes an American icon worth thousands. A letter of invitation to dinner in the hand of Abraham Lincoln is not chopped liver. That letter would likely be valued in thousands of dollars. But make that a personal letter to a friend in which Lincoln expresses remorse about causing so many deaths to keep the Union together, and now we are talking about a note that may be valued in the tens of thousands. Context creates meaning, and a good story fires the imagination.

Of course, the story does not have to be told or even known by the seller. The "story" can reside in the object, to be seen by the knowledgeable collector or dealer. A few years ago, I acquired at auction a box of old pamphlets. Among them was one from the early 1900s advertising a patent medicine. As I leafed through, an ad at the back caught my eye. It was for the Lusitania, which was sailing to England the next month. The date of the ad was April 1917. And now I saw that below the ad was a notice published by the German government that the Lusitania, and other allied ships, were in danger of being fired upon by the German navy, and all passengers should be warned! In this medical pamphlet I had come across an advertisement for the last crossing of the Lusitania, which was sunk by a German sub a few weeks later. I had bought the lot of ephemera for $20. I sold this one piece for $50. The story resided in the object; its previous owner probably didn't take the time to look. These are our FINDS.

FINDS. Those one or two thrilling moments each year that recompense emotionally and financially for hours of frustrating looking and tedious selling. And as knowledge in an area expands, as the number of knowledgeable categories grows, more FINDS are found. We all have sweet stories to tell. My best? I mentioned two at the start of this essay. One was a cloth bag of nearly 70 hand made marbles I bought in Rotterdam for $12. Over the next two years, I sold those marbles, cheaply, for over $600. Another time I traded for an old Pez® dispenser. I gave the equivalent of $15. The man I traded with was European, and he knew the Pez® was a good one. "Don't sell this cheap!" he warned me. Within six months I had sold it for $500. At a show a few years back a man walked up to me and asked $10 for five political pinback buttons. I did not know it at the time, but two of those pinbacks turned out to be valued at $200 each. It happens. Did I cheat somehow, earning this huge profit? Did I take advantage of the ignorance of another? Are there limits to the profits garnered through frontier capitalism?

Values, Ethics, and Moral Obligation

Although in this country, ethics and moral obligation seem as relevant as modesty at the beach, a few words on the subject seem in order.

Seen one way, the flea market is the old west. It is buyer against seller, and seller against seller, in a showdown of wits, knowledge, and connections. If you set yourself up as a dealer, rent a table, and put out items for sale, I do not feel ethically obliged to either educate you or maximize your gain. As a dealer myself, I am in honest and healthy competition with you, and if I have deeper knowledge than you of an item on your table, I do not have to tell you what you have. I may ethically buy it at your price, and even try for a discount. This happens all the time. When I was starting out, I bought an electrical insulator (those glass domes that sit on tops of telephone poles, used to insulate the electrical wire from the ground) for a dollar. A man came to my table and bought it from me for $3. I felt good. 300% profit! Gas for my car for the day! (This was in the 1980s.) This business was fun! Until another man came over a few moments later, and said, "That insulator you just sold? I offered the guy who bought it $50 for it and he turned me down." That insulator was special in a way that I didn't know. How could I? I didn't know insulators. I *still* don't know insulators. But I made my money on that insulator. And someone who *did* know its "story" got a very good deal. There was nothing immoral or unethical about that transaction. It is the dealer's job to educate himself about his merchandise; if he does not do this, the

53

buyer doesn't have to do it for him, and I have no ethical problem with buying an item that is undervalued. I have no trouble with the concept that you get paid for what you know.

Let me hasten to add, I would not do this to a partner or to a friend. My sister also buys and sells collectibles. I would never make a profit off of her. It wouldn't feel right. It would make for bad karma and worse family relations. I have colleagues who are also friends, and experts in areas I know nothing about. My friend Richard knows cufflinks. When I get a set, I show it to him and he tells me the price he would sell it for. He may offer to buy it at some price less than that, and it is up to me to accept his offer or try for the full retail price myself. In return, he comes to me with a political pinback button and I tell him what it is currently trading for, and a lower price at which I would be a buyer. We often sell to each other at a discount, because it is worth our while to do so, but always with full and true disclosure.

This last point is important. If I ask the dealer a question, I expect an honest answer. I often ask is this old? Is it from the period? If he knows that it's old he should tell me; if he knows it's a reproduction or a fantasy, he should say that. (A reproduction is a copy of an original; a fantasy is a new item made in an old style, but it is an item that never before existed, so it can not legitimately be called a re-production.) If he doesn't know whether it is old or not he should say that, too. Whenever I hear this last answer, however, I am suspicious. A dealer who cannot guarantee the authenticity or age of an item may be telling the truth, but he also may be bending his own ethical obligation. (By saying he does not know he is not outright leading me

54

astray.) I have had enough experience with "I don't know" as an answer to generally pass on items when I am not independently sure of their authenticity.

However, it is different again when a non-dealer comes to my table, takes me aside, and shows me an item that has been sitting in the back of his dresser drawer for thirty years, and which he now wishes to sell. This is not someone setting up as a dealer, and I think my ethical obligation is different.

Truthfully, this naïve seller puts me in a bind. Obviously, I want to pay as little as I can. It is easy with another dealer because we are on equal footing, and we each deserve to be paid for whatever it is we know that the other doesn't. But the naïve seller is putting himself at my mercy when he says, "Pay me what you think it's worth." I first tell him that it is in his best interest to do his homework: Research the item, find some price guides, walk the flea markets and try to see what it or a similar item might go for on another table. I tell him that if he does the work, he will get a better price. If he wants to maximize his price, then he needs to go out and get a tax number, rent a table, and sell it himself. If he wants to sell it to me, I might or might not be interested in buying it at all, and if I am interested, I will of course buy it at some wholesale price that will be half or less than half the price I hope to get for the item. If he still wants to sell it to me, after this small lecture, and if I want to buy it, I will now try to do the mental calculation and "create" a price at which I think I can sell this object quickly. This will not be a high-end price for that item, but one, which will be a deal for the collector, and perhaps even a price another dealer would find interesting. And I would then offer this naïve seller half that price. In effect, he would be getting about one-third of the high-end retail price for the object, and about one-half of low-end retail. In creating this price, I am using all my experience and all my instincts. It is far more art than science, and I have made painful mistakes. A lady once approached me with an old leather bucket. It had rivets, and a decal design with a shield and some lions rampant. A very European look. I knew old buckets were valuable, particularly if they were fire buckets, which sold for many hundreds, even thousands of dollars. She assured me that it was 200 years old, and a fire bucket. This is what the dealer who sold it to her assured her. I bought it for $300. I took it to show after show; no one even looked at it. My price came down from $600 to $450 to $350. I was just trying to get my investment back. Still, no interest. I became disenchanted in the extreme. I finally sold it on eBay® for $95. And I was pleased to get that.

But there is another aspect to the ethics and moral obligations of selling at a flea market. Although this country appears much happier with the idea of frontier capitalism, there is also the antiquated notion of a social contract, and, for me, this value carries equal weight. I don't try to take advantage of Barnum's observation that there is a sucker born every minute. I actually want to give fair value to my customers, and I am pleased to have them look and linger and ask questions, even if they have no intention of buying. I take educating as part of my job, and I enjoy sharing what I know. And when I make a sale, if the buyer has a problem with the purchase, I am pleased to take the item back and refund his money.

Because, at the end of the day, I absolutely believe that educating the customer and maintaining a respectable ethical standard means not only a more pleasant work environment, but higher profits as well.

This is interesting. At one and the same time there is an adversarial and a collegial relationship between dealers, and the same is true for vendor and customer. It is part of the majestic complexity of life where contradictory ideas *do* exist side by side. Consider quantum mechanics where light behaves either as a wave or as discrete particles depending on how you design your experiment to measure it. Consider psychoanalytic theory, which tells us love and hate can exist all tangled together in an intimate relationship. (Explosions in both disciplines are common.) So I can visit another dealer who is a friend and say, yes, I am in competition with you, but I am also your colleague who wishes you well and will be of help if I can. And I can have a customer and say, yes, I will make a profit selling this geegaw to you, but you will get fair value, and if you are unhappy with the transaction I will be more considerate of your feelings than my profit. (My goodness, how unAmerican is that! And note, please—this high-mindedness does not extend to the dealer who might buy something from me, shop it around himself, and if he can't make his profit return it to me. That is exploitative, and I keep a baseball bat under my table as a warning to those folks.)

A Word on Nazi, Racist, and Other Offensive Items

This is a delicate subject, and one's moral responsibility is unclear. There are countries where Nazi material is against the law (Germany, Austria, France) and it is illegal for Americans to ship such materials to these countries. We have no such law, but it strikes me that common sense should create guidelines.

There are many categories of items that will offend; Nazi and black racist materials are clearly two. But sexual material (pornographic or merely illustrative) offends sensibilities as well. And we have American anti-semitic material, and American anti-Catholic material. In the last twelve decades we have produced carloads of published materials that have slurred the Chinese, Italians, Germans, Irish, Puerto Ricans, and Mexicans. Virtually every wave of immigrants who landed on our shores, and ended by making America a better and more robust society, has been smeared with negative stereotypes and derogatory material. It is a sad fact that racism, together with religious and ethnic stereotyping, is woven into American history.

However, we are not a nation that forbids owning (or buying and selling) materials that merely offend. Although, as a dealer, you can certainly make your own decision about offering such things, you can not force your morality onto others. I believe that a consensus has emerged along the following lines: that it is the *use* to which the buyer puts the materials that is key. It is repugnant to sell Nazi memorabilia to someone who will use it to glorify the Nazi cause, and I would not knowingly do that. But for a museum or private collector to own such things, and exhibit them with the idea that the world must never forget such madness and horror – that is a legitimate use for these materials. But this is troubling. How do we know someone's mind as he stands at our table fingering a swastika armband that we have for sale, or, for that matter, a star of David taken from a concentration camp victim's shirt. We don't. It is not our value, as Americans, to believe we can know a person's mind from his appearance. It is not our value to even try to peer into a citizen's mind. And it is certainly not our value to create laws that prohibit behavior by presumed intent.

And yet ... and yet ... if you are found with over a certain amount of marijuana or cocaine in your possession, the law does presume intent. You had it not for personal use but for sale, and your punishment is drastically different. If you have a $30,000 annual income and you drive a half million dollar Ferrari, the IRS might become curious and presume that you have unreported income. And in that case it is up to you to show how you bought that car, and not up to them to prove where the income came from.

So, to no one's surprise, and with a nod to Lewis Carroll, the law is what a judge, today, says the law is. There is no hard and fast legal guide here.

For myself, I will not sell pornography as pornography. I have no interest in that. But I do have a first edition of *Screw Magazine*, from 1969, which is pornographic, but also is historically important for affecting the obscenity laws of this country, and this item is for sale. (Only to adults, and I would not prominently display it on my table.) I have no desire to buy or sell Nazi memorabilia, and so much of it has been reproduced that one has to be an expert to know the real from the fake. But I have an avid interest in Holocaust material. As a Jew, I have no trouble selling anti-semitic material because, to my eye, my customers are not purchasing it to support anti-semitic theories, but rather to remind themselves and their children of what the world was once like, and where, in places, it still is. And I have the same attitude towards

59

other racist material, whether directed at African-Americans, Asians, Europeans, or people from Latin-America. (Note: It is comforting to know that members of each of these ethnic groups are among the strongest collectors of historic material that denigrates their own people, for the same reasons that I will buy anti-semitic items.)

And, by the way, this value is not limited to the categories described above. I'm not sure what the law says about this – I expect it varies by county or state – but I won't sell knives or cigarette lighters to teenagers. I think we do have moral obligations in this business, but they are personal, and this, as always, is one price of democracy. As a free country, we must lead by example far more often than we may proscribe by law.

The Discourteous Customer

There are discourteous vendors, and there are discourteous customers. Happily they are a slim minority. Most customers will not bring food into your space and leave a mess. Most smokers will not extinguish their butts under your table. Most will ask permission to open a case. But there is a small percent of us who go through life with a suspicious eye and a sour face. The world is a hostile place to these people, and they find opposition at every turn. As a seller, every customer is a potential thief; as a buyer, every vendor is trying to cheat them. These are impoverished souls who more deserve compassion than anger, and when my energy and patience are high (that is at the beginning of a long day of selling rather than at the end) I treat them gently. All but the most damaged will react well if their suspicions are met with courtesy and respect. Remember, they are looking for reasons *not* to buy. They seek confirmation that the world is a place filled only with predators and prey, where there is no fairness or generosity. If you can take in their negative projectiles, disarm those missiles within yourself, and return something pleasant and positive, some will actually be grateful and you may make a surprise sale. And more often than not at your price!

This happened to me recently. It was at the end of a long July day at Brimfield. I bring to that six day show a comfortable folding beach chair, the kind with straps and armrests, and I sink into it in the afternoon and read my newspaper, even fall asleep in the mid-day sun if all the buyers seem to be at the food court having lunch. My partners bring stiff back chairs with no armrests. Anyway, I am at a table under our tent, attending to a customer, who, after asking a dozen questions, does not buy. So I walk outside the tent where it is sunny and warm, and I find an elderly man with a cane sitting in my chair. He hadn't asked permission. He was tired, he saw an empty chair, and he sat down. Well, I'm tired, too! And this is my chair! But he looks to be eighty years or so, and he *is* carrying a cane. And although no one today would call me a young man, I am still a generation below him. So I pull up one of my partners' stiff back chairs and sit closely next to him, in a friendly yet pointed manner. (I am no stranger to passive-aggressive behavior, but that is another essay.) He begins conversation, taking in the friendliness and ignoring the point, which earns my begrudging respect.

"Warm day," he says. "Yup," I agree. "Hard, walking around these fields." "Um-hmm."

And now I see that his wife is shopping in the tent. She has a wide smile on her face as she takes in my memorabilia, and calls out in a bubbly voice, "Look at this!" She holds up a small radio from the 1940s. "Remember?" He does. She happily reminisces about several more items, and it is clear to me that she is only marking time so her husband can rest.

As I resign myself to being a public facility, he begins conversing again and I am surprised to learn that he lost his wife thirteen years ago. I sit more attentively as he tells me he met this cheerful lady at the senior home, just two years before, and that last year they went to Europe – the first trip abroad for either of them. The scene is transformed for me. All my irritation is gone, and I feel awash with a spirit of generosity. I am delighted that this senior, who acknowledges that he is indeed eighty-five, is sitting in my chair. His companion comes over and hears us talking about their trip, and she cannot help but plunge into an amusing story about their troubles with an Italian taxi driver. They laugh and relive the memory, and with a small start I realize that they have brought me out of the world of "private treaty," where business is done, and into the world of "social contract." It only lasts for a moment, but what a nice moment it is. And as I look back, today, I am grateful to them.

Note: I have several times mentioned Brimfield. Brimfield is a town in south-central Massachussetts, on Route 20 a few miles west of Sturbridge, and three times a year it becomes a Mecca for those with a passion for antiques and collectibles. For six days in May, July, and September, a mile long strip of pastures just west of the town is transformed into a dozen antique and collectible shows; each one, looking like an army encampment of tents and tables and vehicles, is home to hundreds of vendors. They have quaint names: Dealer's Choice, Heart-of-the-Mart, New England Motel, J & J (also called "The Sisters"), and my own home at Quaker Acres. By the end of the six days, thousands of sellers and tens of thousands of buyers from around the world have exchanged greetings, stories, and emptied or filled their wallets as they trade – well – everything: trash, treasure, junk, heirlooms. It is all there, all part of Brimfield.

Preparedness:
A Final Checklist

All right, you are now knowledgeable, ethically armed, and ready to do flea market combat. Some final words before the fray.

Know your customers. You will have lookers, pickers, collectors, fellow dealers, and children. They all deserve courtesy and respect, but they do not all equally deserve your time. You are interested in making a sale, and when the inevitable ancient mariner comes to your table to tell you all about the collections of his youth, keep your eyes sharp and excuse yourself politely when a woman who looks like a dealer begins picking out two or three pieces for serious consideration.

Note: One can sell to dealers, and quite well, because, if you have something in their area of interest, they are no longer dealers but the most avid of collectors. And if your item is truly rare, you will get the best price. I have a wonderful example. I went to Europe a few years back and bought a little box with an ivory swivel on top. Under the swivel were signs for the four suits in a deck of cards: hearts, diamonds, clubs, and spades. This was some sort of trump marker. It was old, from the end of the 18th Century, and inside the box were thin bone strips each colored with a heart, a diamond, a club, or a spade. This box was used with a card game; I'm not sure that anyone today knows exactly which. I bought the piece in Beaune, France, at a show, from a dealer, for $54. I took it to a show in Allentown, PA, and put it in my case. Before the show opened, the dealer in the next booth noticed it and asked about it. I explained what I knew. It turned out that she was one of the more advanced collectors of games in the country, and one of her specialties was trump markers. Within five minutes I sold it to her for $300. I was lucky; she was one of the very few people who would have paid my price for that item. She was a dealer of other games, but this was going into her collection. Where else was she going to find another 18th Century trump marker like that? I had made her day, and she had made mine.

It is important to mentally prepare for the inevitable negotiation. Of course, it is a matter of personal choice, but I try to not lose a sale even if the price is a little lower than the one I would like to get. I have come up with a companion slogan to "Buy Low, Sell High." It is, "Buy Slow, Sell Fast." By this I mean take your time when you are buying. Look the item over carefully. Consider what you might sell it for, and how easy or hard that sale might be. At the same time, if someone makes you an offer for an item you have had on your table for a year, and that offer is 10% below the price you wanted, say "thank you very much" and grab the money with both hands!

You can add tax to the item, or tell your customers it is included in the final price. I much prefer the latter. There is something unsavory about going through a negotiation with a customer, and then, when it is over, adding tax to the final price. Do the calculations in your head in advance. If you are going to pay 6% tax on the item to your State Government, include that in the tag price and, mentally, in the final price you will accept.

Have a receipt book. Use it if you have that discipline. It's one way to keep track of what you sold. But even if you don't use it regularly, there will be customers who will need receipts.

If you do not yet have a computer with email, and you wish to be in this business, get on line! Collectors and dealers are already doing much business over the internet, and this will only grow. There can be more to this business than making sales on the weekend, during the good weather, at flea markets or shows. You will be meeting people all the time, forming relationships for buying and selling. The internet, with email, has made communication astonishingly quick, simple, and cheap. With email, these relationships can provide sales even on a Tuesday or Wednesday or Thursday in the middle of January, when the snow is a foot high outside your door.

Have a business card made up and give it out. It will make you feel legitimate, and give your customers confidence. Make certain your email address is on your card, together with your tax ID number.

Take checks! I didn't at first and met with outraged longtime collectors who only paid that way. Of course I didn't know them; I didn't know anyone. If you are selling an item for hundreds and hundreds of dollars, you might want to ask for part cash part check. If you are selling an item for a thousand dollars, I think it is legitimate to treat it the way you would an eBay® sale—hold the item until the check clears and then ship it. But for less expensive items, a check is fine. I have been in business for 15 years and I have taken many hundreds of checks. I have been ripped off just once.

A Taxonomy of value.

What's It Worth?

Value (or worth) is not price. Value is the degree to which an object is desired. Price is the means by which we quantify that value. Oscar Wilde crisply defined a cynic as one who knew the price of everything and the value of nothing.

This chapter is not a price guide. Instead, it is an attempt to list and understand some principles by which we place value on objects. By understanding these principles, we minimize the arbitrariness of picking a price, we can apply a defendable price, and we have a basis for arguing a competitor's haphazard price.

A customer approaches my table, looks around with interest, and checks the price of a Prince Albert tobacco tin ($6). He comments to no one in particular, "I have twenty of those in my basement. I didn't know I was rich."

Another looks at an early comic book in mint condition. "When I was a kid, I had a thousand of these," he says. "I don't know what happened. My mother must have thrown them out."

A woman regards my display of old cobalt medicine bottles. "I've got a bottle just like that one at home. What's it worth?"

What's it worth.

The man with the Prince Albert tins makes the common mistake of thinking that worth resides only within the object. If I have a $6 price on a Prince Albert tin prominently displayed on my table at the Triple Pier Show—which is located in the middle of Manhattan, where I pay $800 for two days of exhibiting and where the promoters of the show spend thousands advertising it so that customers the world over attend—he believes that the $6 price applied to my tin should equally apply to each of his Prince Alberts sitting on his basement shelf in Brooklyn.

The man with the comic books is probably aware that his wistful memory is naïve. If our mothers hadn't trashed our comics they would be plentiful today, and not worth much. Better to put the question in prospect. Let him declare which 10¢ item of today (okay, with inflation, which dollar item) should be saved because it will be worth hundreds of dollars fifty years from now? And, of course, if we all land on the same future collectible it will be worthless.

Which brings us to an important point. Merchandise created today for the collectibles market, such as items produced by the Franklin Mint, are a reasonable bet to not increase much in value. Collectors are a contrary lot. They value stuff produced in an unselfconscious manner that truly represents an era past. They take delight in assigning an aesthetic and a high sticker price to such trivial objects of daily life as children's toys or tavern foam scrapers (they look like doctor's tongue depressors, and were used in bars to take the heads off glasses of beer).

The woman with the cobalt bottles is asking the question in everyone's mind, the one I hear at every show. "I have this Howdy Doody lamp from my childhood." "I went to a ball game and my son got a Tom Seaver bobble-head doll." "I have a collection of old straight razors." "What's it worth?"

If it is early in the day and I am not tired, and the questioner is polite, I try to answer as fully as I can. I begin by saying I cannot create a price for his collectible object. Yes, create a price. Collectibles dealers do not "quote" prices the way stockbrokers do. We have no exchange that makes a market. We do not stamp a standard mark-up retail price on cellophane-wrapped packages the way a supermarket manager does to bread. We *create* our prices based on a number of variables. Many of these variables belong to the object itself such as rarity and condition. Other variables reside in the environment outside of the collectible such as how many people collect that category of item, what era it represents and how popular that era is today, and how and where it is displayed. And a third equally important set of variables reside in me as the dealer – how much I paid for it, how long I've had it, what my cash concerns are at this moment, even how much I truly love or hate it.

To determine the first set of variables, those that are part of the object, I use my experience. I think of the times I've seen this object before, what price other dealers put on it, and what it actually sold for. Perhaps I check a current price guide, or auction result. I might ask another dealer more experienced in the category what he thought.

The second set of variables, those that belong to the environment around the collectible, is more abstract than the first and harder to quantify. In America today, baseball is more collected than soccer; a medal commemorating Hank Aaron will probably sell faster, and for more money, than one commemorating Pele. The reverse is true in Europe. A piece of Steuben glass, sold in a country flea market in Nebraska, will likely not get the price it could achieve if placed in a shop on Rodeo Drive in Los Angeles. The third set of variables is unique to the seller, and are mostly unanalyzed, but they are quickly and certainly felt.

The questioner thinks he is asking me, the "expert," to

tell him the objective worth of his treasure – a price he might realize if he wanted to sell it tomorrow. To whom he might sell it, and how he might learn of and contact that willing buyer, are questions he does not consider. Instead he is asking me to create a price, sight unseen.

What I can do for the questioner is offer a price range based on general variables that I know from experience. In the case of the man commenting on my tobacco tin, I can tell him that this Prince Albert is a common one. In poor condition it is worthless, while in excellent condition $6 is about as much as it should bring. I could also tell him that even if his tin cans were in mint condition, he could not sell them to me. I have enough Prince Alberts, and when I sell this one I am not eager to buy another. Both our tins may be exactly the same, but they are worth $6 only when they find a customer, and which of us has a better chance of doing that? This begins to answer the question of which of the two tins might be *worth* $6.

In these answers, I find myself talking about all the variables mentioned above, and more, including how much time and energy the owner is willing to invest in selling his collectible. Clearly this answer was not what my question-ers had in mind. They wanted concrete figures which, presumably, they could turn into cash; this I could not provide. And as my answers grew more abstract, and took more time, I began to think I should write a page or two as a handout, to give to the interested public. But as I contemplated that task, I realized the essay would not be brief. The question was everything but simple. Also, at its nub, it was not unimportant. And so this small book was born.

Upon reflection, I decided there were two global categories for determining worth. One is value that attaches to the object itself. The other is value that attaches to the environment around the object, (which would include the "human environment," those personal variables that are within the buyer and the seller).

OBJECT VALUES: Values that attach to the object itself.

INTRINSIC VALUE: This is the bedrock of all principles of value. In our economic system, the items of intrinsic value are the precious metals. Gold has a precise intrinsic value that is expressed in terms of national currencies, which have no intrinsic value themselves, (hence gold's value "increases" in times of inflation). But gold has only relative intrinsic value. It is valuable by convention, and its worth fluctuates on the open market. One could argue that the only items of absolute intrinsic value (and absolute only to us poor humans) are items that aid in survival: food when we are hungry, water when we are thirsty, and clothing and shelter to protect us from the elements. In collecting, the intrinsic values of the materials used to make the object, precious metals and gemstones, give the item a base value that can easily be realized.

Note: Since objects with a high intrinsic value, such as gold rings, are easy to sell, these items are much more prone to be shoplifted than other collectibles. So seller beware.

USE VALUE: Items are valued because they are useful. If you wish to open a bottle of wine, the finest hammer is of no worth. Nothing will do but a corkpull. (Cork*screws* are but one type of corkpull – there are other designs such as one that uses compressed air to remove the cork, and another that uses two thin, flexible metal prongs that slip between cork and bottle neck and rotate the cork out.) And as long as you need one in your kitchen, why not make it an aesthetically pleasing one, which in many cases is sturdier and more functional than its modern counterpart?

HISTORIC VALUE: Items that are important in history are valued for that reason alone. And when we value them highly enough, we put them in museums. An Eighteenth Century document may have value for its scarcity, or for the aesthetics of the calligraphy, but if it is our original Declaration of Independence, its value is incalculable.

TOTEMIC VALUE: This is a local, individualized cousin to Historic Value. Just as some of our native population believed that the spirits of their ancestors resided in totem poles, which then became sacred objects, today an object can acquire value based on similar personal association. A celebrity autograph is a pure example of totemic value – it has value only through the celebrity who penned her name. (If it's a fake it has no value whatsoever.) In 1996, a set of President Kennedy's golf clubs fetched over $750,000 at auction. The buyer, Arnold Schwarzenneger, who is married to Maria Shriver (President Kennedy's niece) paid that price because he wanted to own *that* set of clubs. The example cited above, our Declaration of Independence, has enormous totemic value because, I think quite literally, the spirit of America is felt to live within it.

There are, actually, two levels of totemic value. There are items that were once owned or used by a notable person, and gain value through association. But there are also items that were actually *part* of the person. In the first case, the uniform that Bobby Bonds wore when he hit his 73rd home run might sell for the price of a down payment on a small house. Similarly, today, Presidents will use ten or twenty pens to sign an important document. These pens are handed out to the dignitaries present, and become valuable mementos of that day. But items that actually were *part* of a person have the most powerful totemic value. A lock of hair is a popular example of that. The autograph is a part of a person, extruded through handwriting, as is a personal letter or a diary, which also contain thoughts. An original photo captures the person entire at one unique moment. A Saint's relic might be a snippet of that Saint's actual clothing, or, more graphically, a fragment of bone. These letters and photos and relics are powerful totemic legacies, and are highly valued for the feeling of having a piece of the person with us.

AUTHORSHIP: This is another cousin to both Historic and Totemic Value, and it is seen more often in the world of fine art and antiques than in my world of collectibles. Part of the charm of collectibles is that they were items of every day life, anonymously produced, never thought of as art and rarely signed. But one's great grandfather might have acquired a Civil War photo, which would not have had great cash value a hundred years ago, but today would be prized. However, if by chance this photo came from the studio of Matthew Brady, this would no longer be a simple collectible. The authorship would make this an important photograph, one that would be sought after by advanced collectors and museums, and it would carry a price to reflect that stature.

AESTHETIC VALUE: The marriage of quality materials to exquisite design. An elegant blend of form and function. Masterful craftsmanship. How the item strikes the eye. No value is more subjective than the aesthetic, and few play a greater role in establishing price. Which is why developing one's eye to spot the single beautifully made item on a table of junk is, perhaps, the most important skill a new vendor can acquire.

Aesthetic value, however, is subject to fads. Today, lamps and furniture from the 1950s are in demand. Twenty years ago this was not the case, and twenty years from now it may not be the case, again. "Kitch" is a relatively recent aesthetic idea. "Kitch" holds that items produced in an especially garish, outrageous, and/or tacky manner have value for those very qualities. My wife, Susan, who has historically been an excellent picker for me, recently drove to her aunt's house and brought home a trunk full of things that her aunt was giving away. One item was so tacky that she almost didn't take it, but her aunt implored, and she gave in. It was a McCoy pineapple cookie jar, and Susan thought it was embarrassingly ugly. Needless to say, that was the only collectible in the carload that I could easily sell.

That being said, the market does seem to hold for the great names that define an era and an aesthetic. Art nouveau will wax and wane in the popular taste; Tiffany will not. The 1950s will someday go out of style. But an Eames chair will most likely continue to command a high price from the serious furniture collector.

It is interesting to learn the ways in which these values interact with one another. The celebrity autograph mentioned above for its totemic value has an aesthetic one as well. If the autograph is bold and beautifully penned, it will be more valued than one dashed off by the same celebrity in a scratchy and less legible hand. If a theatre star has signed a show program, the autograph will have more value on the cover, where the owner can easily frame and display it, than on an inner page. And if the entire Broadway cast of, say, the original production of "South Pacific" signed the front of their program, with Mary Martin as one of the group, that program might be *less* valuable than one signed only by Ms. Martin in large bold hand. The addition of lesser-known actors does not increase the price, while Mary Martin fans will much prefer the larger, more visible signature.

RARITY: The principle most people believe has the greatest effect in creating value in antiques and collectibles. But rarity, or scarcity, can be overrated. To truly add value, the object must be rare in a significant manner. I owned a mechanical device that looked like a small washing machine ringer for a full year. It could have fit into a six-inch square box, and since I'd never seen one before, I thought it might be a salesman's sample. In the time that I owned it, only one visitor had claimed to have set eyes on another, and this woman told me the device was a pea-shucker – one places the pea between the pair of rollers, turns the handle, and the rollers squeeze the pod, forcing out the peas. Well, maybe so. As stories go, this was a good one. In any event, this was a genuinely rare item, priced at a reasonable $25, yet for years no one bought it. People smiled when they learned what I thought it was, but no one was interested in putative pea-shuckers, no matter how rare. On the other hand, there are many thousands of stamp collectors in the world. Any truly rare stamp, such as one with a printing mistake, will be desired by a large number of people and see a drastic increase in price. In the collectible world, commonness is a curse. Rarity by itself is interesting, but must be mated to a desire for the object to affect price.

NOVELTY/CURIOSITY: The intrigue factor. This is related to rarity, but in a personal way. If you haven't seen something, it is rare to you, and therefore interesting, especially if it works through a novel principle. A folding ruler is not even scarce, but if one has never seen the cleverness of the design, one is surprised, and marvels at how it unfolds and folds. Tin toys that windup and move in unexpected ways, or mechanical banks that deposit a coin in some quick and clever manner gain value because they are startling and amusing novelties. When I did sell the pea-shucker, it went to someone as impressed with its novelty as I was.

CONDITION: *The* value held with uncompromising vigor by collectors. If it is made of ceramic or glass, is there the smallest chip or flaw anywhere? If made of tin, does the item betray more than a speck of rust? If paper, are there slight tears, folds, feathering at the corners? With antique furniture or lamps, original finishes are critical. Prices will be halved or worse if an old bronze lamp has lost its original patina and has been shined up, or if a Colonial era table has been stripped of its original paint and refinished. The same is true of coins. I remember when I was ten years old I took a wad of steel wool to my coin collection of Indian head pennies and buffalo nickels and liberty dimes and made them sparkle; my mother was so proud. But this value of condition has been carried to absurd heights. In the heyday of the baseball card mania, a Mickey Mantle rookie card, in mint condition, might have been offered at $800. Let the potential buyer point out that one of the corners was just barely feathered and the asking price might have dropped to $80.

As mentioned above, it is useful to understand the relationships between these variables. Forgiveness of condition is a function of rarity. That is, the rarer an item, the more willing the collector will be to overlook some flaws and buy it, with the hope to later find a better example, and "trade up"—that is, he will later buy a second one, in better condition, and hope to trade or sell the first.

A NOTE on cleaning and mending: Since condition is critical, cleaning or repairing collectibles is tricky business, and a novice should take the same oath that doctors take: First, do no harm. As we have already discussed, certain antiques gain the greater part of their value from *never* having been cleaned; the original finish, or the patina that formed over the years, is highly desired by collectors. That having been said, you will learn when judicious cleaning will improve some items and lead to faster sales with better prices. Most silver does not gain from being tarnished. A brass bound folding ruler will benefit from some of the corrosion removed, and the brass edges shined. I find that when I do clean metal, a very fine steel wool, such as #000, does not leave scratch marks and handles the job nicely. If I pick up a rusty metal bottle opener I bathe it in WD-40 for a few days, then apply the fine steel wool. Not all the rust comes off, but the bottle opener looks much better. Be gentle with paper and cardboard. Never mend paper with cellophane tape, which cannot be removed without tearing. If you need to mend paper, a special document tape is made that can be applied and removed without causing further damage. Post cards or advertising trade cards that have been glued into an album can be soaked out. But ask questions first of an ephemera dealer, and make your first attempts on cards that are not valuable. Any vendor who blithely thumbs a self-stick price marker onto a paper or cardboard collectible should be shot. These self-stick circles and rectangles can not be removed without leaving a tear in the paper or an awful sticky stain. To price a deck of cards, take a small plain piece of paper, write the price on it, and insert it into the pack. Most small pieces of ephemera can go in plastic holders, which not only protects them, but allows you to put a sticky price marker on the plastic instead of on the collectible. It is the custom to use a light pencil mark on the back of postcards to indicate price. But only a pencil that is easily erasable, and, of course, never a pen!

SIZE AND WEIGHT: I was once offered an upright piano for a $100. The piano was clearly worth much more than that, but the piano was in New Haven, Connecticut, my apartment was in New York City, and my apartment was a one-room studio. I had to decline the offer. In this new century, more and more Americans are living in cities, and in apartments. Space is an issue, and transporting large, heavy items usually incurs an expense. So people are collecting smaller, lighter things. As a dealer, one can accommodate this trend, or not. Personally, I have specialized in "smalls": Pinback buttons, little bottles, sample medicine and tobacco tins, advertising trade cards, cigar cutters, figural pencil sharpeners, fruit knives, eye cups, shaving equipment, photographs. In this world of collectibles, small is good and smaller is better. And in any category, true miniatures can command the highest prices of all.

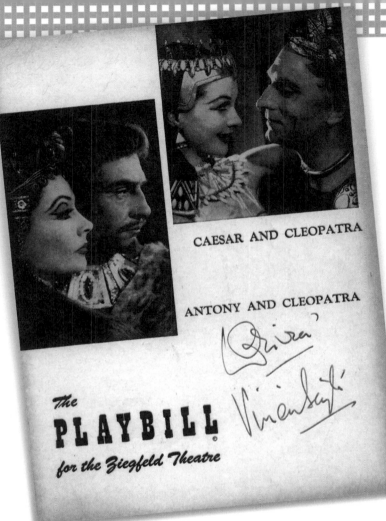

CAESAR AND CLEOPATRA

ANTONY AND CLEOPATRA

The
PLAYBILL
for the Ziegfeld Theatre

The theatre program for "Caesar and Cleopatra" and "Antony and Cleopatra," already unusual in that it represents two plays performed by the same cast, achieves a high totemic value by the autographs of the stars, Sir Lawrence Olivier and Vivien Leigh. Although in this book I have made the point that a single autograph on a program is more valued than multiple signings, here is an exception to the rule. Both Olivier and Leigh were not only huge stars, they were married. This program, representing the pair's tour de force, presenting both Shaw's and Shakespeare's versions of the Caesar/Antony/Cleopatra story, is enhanced by having both signatures. Normally, Sir Lawrence's autograph would sell for something less than $100; Ms. Leigh's would sell for over $200. If I had this item at an advertised auction, I would start the bidding at $300, and not be surprised if it went for more than that.

Advertising trade cards were popular in the late 1800s. These postcard-sized pieces of art were used to inform the public about all sorts of products and services, and were widely collected in albums, even then. Pictured above is a rare card advertising State Line Passenger Steamships, a transatlantic ship company that brought immigrants to America. The image shows Castle Garden, an island in New York Harbor where immigrants were received before Ellis Island was built. This card is in very good condition, and because of the intricate image and historical value would most likely sell for over $100.

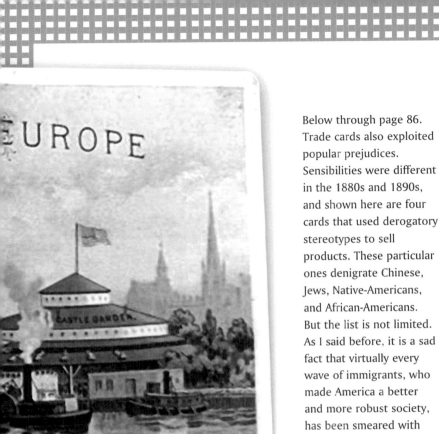

Below through page 86. Trade cards also exploited popular prejudices. Sensibilities were different in the 1880s and 1890s, and shown here are four cards that used derogatory stereotypes to sell products. These particular ones denigrate Chinese, Jews, Native-Americans, and African-Americans. But the list is not limited. As I said before, it is a sad fact that virtually every wave of immigrants, who made America a better and more robust society, has been smeared with negative stereotypes and derogatory images.

THE PRINTER FIEND WHO RUNS THE ELEPHANTINE PRESS

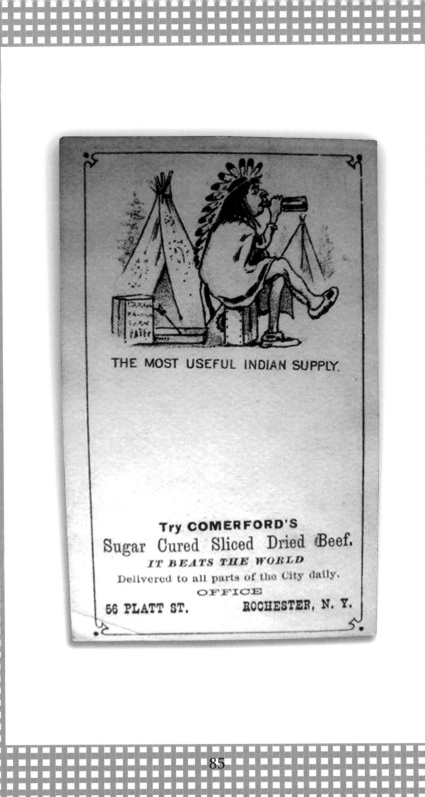

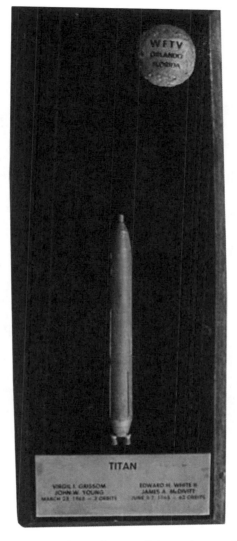

TITAN

VIRGIL I. GRISSOM
JOHN W. YOUNG
MARCH 23, 1965 — 3 ORBITS

EDWARD H. WHITE II
JAMES A. McDIVITT
JUNE 3-7, 1965 — 62 ORBITS

I suppose every human endeavor is part of history. but our Space Program is in the first rank of our nation's achievement. Anything original to the 1960s Space effort is strongly collected. Above we have a plaque put out by WFTV, a tv station in Orlando Florida. The plaque commemorates the Titan rocket, and the 1965 space flights of Grissom and Young in March of that year, and White and McDivitt in June. A collectible like this, with few (if any) others around, is difficult to value. But its history, together with its rarity should put the price above $100.

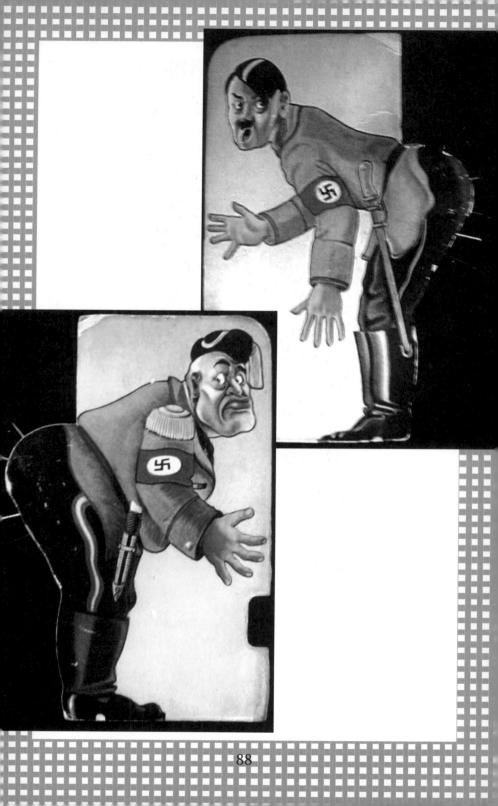

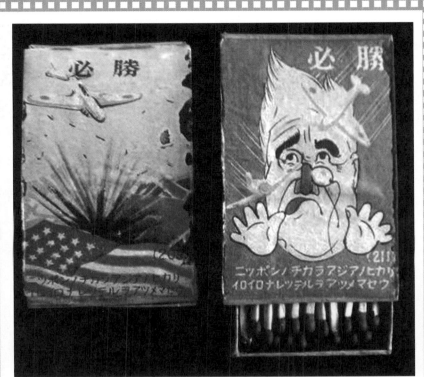

History is always collected, and the two items on the opposite page came out of World War 2. The images of Hitler and Mussolini are the front and back of one cardboard piece, that is actually a pincushion! Yes, there is a thin strip of cushioning just where it ought to be; you can see the pins sticking out. I'm sure this novelty provided a few smiles during the grim early 1940s. In this piece we see a joining of history, aesthetics, and use, together with a little wit, and this item today would fetch well over $100. The two World War 2 matchboxes are equally colorful, but here the price is in the story. These objects were created in Japan during World War 2, and show anti-American images, (that's FDR on the right, being harried by Japanese war planes). Japanese propaganda pieces, like this, are far rarer than American ones, and in fact I haven't seen other matchboxes like these two, so I truly don't know how to price them. But even in less than pristine condition, at $150 each I would not consider them expensive.

I have grown very fond of pinback buttons for two reasons. First, because they are small and light and don't break, which makes them easy to collect and to sell. Second, because they include so many areas of collecting. A political collector might buy a button from me, but so will a movie fan, or a collector of ice cream items or cowboys or sports memorabilia. Here are three social cause pins from the 1960s, against the Vietnam War. If you saw these pins at a show you could expect to pay $20 to $50 each for them.

In all areas of collecting there are reproductions and fantasies. (A reproduction is a copy of an original design; a fantasy is an item that may look old, but in fact has never been produced before.) Shown here are two Shirley Temple pins. The smaller one is an original, from the 1930s, and in very good condition. It will normally sell for over $100. The larger one was not produced when Shirley was a child. It was made in the last twenty years or so, and would be valued at less than $5.

Reproductions and Fantasies are even more worrisome in political collecting. Above is a tray of bogus political pins. None are marked in any way to let the viewer know it is not a genuine campaign item, and even experienced dealers may be fooled. These pins are considered to have no value, and in fact they are forbidden from being exhibited at all responsible political shows. There is good reason for this. The original Al Smith pin, shown upper left, ("Al and Joe Let's Go") would sell for several hundred dollars. If I sold this fake for $10 or $20, I would have no guarantee that down the line some unscrupulous vendor might try pass it off as the real thing. As with counterfeit money, once these pins are identified as frauds they should be taken out of circulation.

But not all pinback buttons are expensive; most in fact are easily affordable. Pictured here in this 'butterfly tray' are about 40 political buttons, dating from the 1930s to the 1980s. They are common pins, but still very nice for a beginning collection, and would sell for $1 to $5 each.

A photo of several of the fields at Brimfield, taken from a low flying plane. Brimfield, in south-central Massachusetts, continues to be the largest show in the North-East, drawing serious dealers and collectors alike.

The beautiful ceramic 1964 New York's World Fair ashtray might be priced at $50 or more. But did you notice the repaired crack on the upper right corner? When buying glass or ceramic, it is often more useful to use your hands than your eyes. Run a fingertip around all edges, feeling for the tell-tale jag of a chip. In this condition this ashtray should be priced closer to $15 than $50.

Environmental Values

Environmental values do not reside directly in the object, but reflect the environment around the object. This is a large and complicated idea, and the notion encompasses a wide range of values. For instance, the *macro-environment* includes place and time in the largest sense, both of which will affect the value of your collectibles. The *local environment* considers the specific show or flea market in which you are selling, even down to the set-up on your table. And of course there is the *human environment*, which looks at all the ways in which people interact with objects — what they buy, why they buy, and how much they are willing to pay.

MACRO-ENVIRONMENT: The macro-environment consists of several features:

Place: are you selling in Ames Iowa or in the center of Chicago?

Economics: Is there a recession, or is the economy booming? How is the dollar doing relative to the yen and to the Euro?

Time: Certain decades and styles are in fashion while others are not. There may be demographic reasons for this.

Perception of Collectibles: Is the entire business of collectibles (and antiques) hot or has it cooled off. What is the public awareness of this business?

These questions are related to the macro-environment and will affect your business, sometimes markedly.

PLACE: We've all heard the joke: What are the three most important things to look for when buying commercial real estate? Answer: Location, Location, and Location. People expect to pay a high price for an art deco lamp if they walk into a shop in South Beach, Miami. They know nothing there will be cheap. But expectations for buying that same lamp run quite differently a few hundred miles north, shopping a flea market in rural Georgia. Based on expectation alone, collectibles will bring different prices in different locations. (And high rents for vendors are based on something other than whimsy.)

THE ECONOMY: Here is an example of the economic macro-environment. In the 1990s, I had a small collectibles shop on 25th Street in New York City. In the middle of that decade, I would estimate half of my business came from foreigners – Europeans and Asians. The Japanese, in particular, were avid collectors of Americana. They were middle-aged men, alone or with their wives, probably here in New York on business. Most spoke no English, they just quietly came into my shop, nodded politely, looked around for a few minutes, then pointed to this, this, this, this, and that. And I would make a pile: an old Coca-Cola® knife, a sample tobacco tin, a 19th Century photograph of a baseball player, a Zippo® cigarette lighter. I would write down the tag price of each item, add the total, then cross it out and write a price 20% lower. They would nod and smile and take out crisp $100 bills, still fresh from the bank. Not a word was exchanged, but business was done. Then, one day, the yen collapsed. It was like an eclipse of the sun. The next week my business suffered, and I didn't see another Japanese customer for the rest of the time I owned that shop.

Today, the major economies are struggling. America has suffered three blows, each one driving the economy down or keeping it from recovering. We saw a stock market reversal, which featured a Nasdaq crash. We were hit by 9/11, and the emotional and financial costs of a war on terrorism. And most recently we have witnessed the spate of corporate scandals, led by the Enron fraud, with major corporate leaders being indicted and put on trial. People are a little more fearful and a lot less trustworthy – as a nation we feel somewhat poorer. Surely there is less economic expansion now; we are trying to hold onto what we have.

All this translates to less disposable income to buy antiques and collectibles. I hear it from vendors at all the shows: Business is down.

Still, as I write this, America is riding out the storm. Unemployment is up, but only by a little. Vendors are having to adjust their expectations – they are not seeing the sales they saw in the high-rolling Nineties – but most are still making some sort of living. The macro-environment for this business today is still good, and the popular culture reflects this (the PERCEPTION OF COLLECTIBLES is strongly and positively held in the general public). The "Antiques Road Show" has a solid TV audience, and has spawned half a dozen imitators; eBay® is going strong and has created a worldwide buzz. When the U.S. economy recovers, prices of collectibles will once again rise. But be wary. All economics is cyclical. When the United States has a more serious, more sustained economic downturn, and drags Europe along for the plunge, antiques and collectibles will suffer. Cash will be king, again. And bargains once more will be there for the taking.

That being said, the very best of antiques and collectibles rarely suffer much loss of value during economic downturns, and if they do, it is temporary. The poor will always be with us, but so will the rich. All the owner of a Van Gogh needs at an auction is two very wealthy people who would kill to have his painting.

TIME: In the narrow sense, the time of year counts. The national buying frenzy we go through between Thanksgiving and Christmas, when malls do half their yearly business, can bring robust sales at collectibles shows as well. (Hard to have outdoor flea markets in most parts of this country at that time of year.) This spree continues into January, when folks cash their year-end bonuses. But business dies in February, as we begin paying off our credit card balances, and generally doesn't pick up again at least until after taxes are paid on April 15.

But in a wider sense, time counts in a different way. One would think there would be a straight line of increasing value as a collectible aged, but this is not the case. Eras go in and out of fashion, and there is a demographic theory for this. People like to collect stuff from their childhood. But think for a minute. When you are 15 or 20 years old you have no interest in your childhood, except to escape it and set yourself up as an adult. When you are 25 to 35 you are making your way in a career, beginning a family perhaps. At 35-45 you are consolidating your life and your career, paying off a mortgage, maybe you are sending children to college, ponying up for weddings. A number of us are beginning second marriages or starting a second career, paying alimony and child support. In any event, many of us still don't have much disposable income. But consider our lives as we enter our 50s. For the most part, we are where we are going to be. We make our peace with the expectations of our youth, and, as recompense for lost ideals and evaporated dreams, we are making decent incomes. For the first time, we are not paying for braces or tuition; we can buy for ourselves. We acquire second homes, we support mid-life crises with sports cars and motorcycles and sailboats, we travel more. We have disposable income, and we can indulge ourselves. We are also looking ahead to old age, and the shocking thought occurs that we are not immortal. So childhood memories become important, and some of us begin to collect the objects that made those memories. If this analysis has truth, then at any point in time we would see a wave of buying interest in the decade forty years earlier. And in fact that is my experience. As the 1990s began, the 1950s became hot; prices for furniture and lamps, even toys from that decade, zoomed. Now, as the 21st Century dawns, we have a surge of interest in the 1960s. Mementos from the movement against the Vietnam War, and from the social turbulence of those hippie years, are commanding high prices. And at the same time, items from the 1930s languish, probably because there are fewer folks around who remember that decade; and those who do are now in their seventies-plus and more concerned about paying for prescription medicines than buying an NRA poster. Collectibles go up in price and down in price as the numbers of people who desire them, and can afford them, increases and decreases.

Local Environment

YOUR FLEA MARKET: Is your flea market or show well attended? Does it have a traditional following, or is it being well publicized now? Are there a number of other vendors who also sell collectibles, or is this flea market really a glorified yard sale? If all your fellow vendors are selling hats and belts and scarves, you will find that dealers and collectors of collectibles won't even show up. This is not the market for you.

My own experience with the local environment occurred mostly during the five years I ran my collectibles shop in New York City. It was in the Chelsea Antiques Building, on West 25th Street in Manhattan, overlooking the 6th Avenue flea market. As I've already mentioned, the 90s were a high point for that market. Collectibles were suddenly "in." My shop was just a room, really, 8 x 16 feet, on the fourth floor, but it sat on a corner and had windows with great light. I furnished it with glass table-tops and shelves – no closed cases – everything out in the open to be picked up and looked at and touched. Finally, I could put out paper and cardboard items, and buy both weightier and more fragile things, since I would not be packing and unpacking all the time, moving my wares to the flea markets and shows.

Using only my best judgment, and with much help from friends, I considered all the variables to make my "local environment" as attractive and as functional as possible. I was fortunate with natural daylight, but I put in halogen lamps for those winter afternoons when it is dark at 4:00 PM. I made sure shelves were not too high for small people to reach, but that breakable items were well away from children's hands. When I ordered the glass table tops, I had the corners rounded, for safety. I grouped my collections together – pinback buttons on one table, bottles on a set of shelves against the window where blue and green and red glass could glow in the morning sun. My metal ware had another table. Nutcrackers and bottle openers and corkscrews, letter openers paperweights and paper clips. Enough to give a wide choice of prices and styles, but not a number to confuse. Having this shop made me more aware than ever that *I* was my business. How I selected and presented my merchandise; how I greeted my customers; how I tried to educate them about my items (if they needed education; in many cases they educated me); how I made them comfortable when they did not buy; the guarantees of authenticity I offered plus a return policy— all this meant that people would either get into the elevator of that building and ride it to the 4th floor to see my shop, or they would not.

About my return policy: If a customer wanted to return an item he had purchased, and if it was in the same condition as when he purchased it, I bought it back. For the same price, and for cash. I don't know, but I suspect this policy resulted in more sales than I would otherwise have had. I do know that during the five years I maintained the shop, I only had a handful of returns. Most vendors don't do this, and I understand why. In fact, I do not state this policy so openly now when I do flea markets and shows. My customers can't find me as easily, and I don't know them as well. Nevertheless, if within any reasonable period of time a customer who I know comes back with an item he has bought from me, and is now dissatisfied, and if he hasn't damaged the item in any way and we both remember what he paid, I will still refund his money. Goodwill is worth more than any sale.

WEATHER AND HOLIDAYS: What's the weather like today? If it's a perfect spring day, your outdoor flea market will be packed. But if it's too hot, too cold, or rainy, and you are selling outside, you are in for a long, uncomfortable day. However, if you are selling at an indoor show, bad weather is usually a plus. People want somewhere to go on the weekend, and rainy or snowy days can see a swell of indoor shoppers. For obvious reasons, the month between Thanksgiving and Christmas is a very good time for selling, while particular holidays have their own characteristics. Mother's Day, for example, is usually not a good day to sell. Your customers are having brunch with Mom, and unless Mom is a collector, they won't be visiting you. The same used to be true for Super-Bowl Sunday, but since they moved the Big Game into the early evening, selling can be good that morning and early afternoon.

NEATNESS: What does your table look like? Does it show a sense of order? Do you use a tablecloth, or throw your merchandise on the raw tabletop? These are personal preferences, but can also be part of a business model. I have heard dealers say that the flea market public wants a sense of disorder, even chaos. This theory has it that people want to treasure hunt; they want to believe that you, the vendor, don't know your merchandise, and you are just throwing stuff on a table. Well, maybe. But the proof is not in the presentation but the price. When I have to dig through a cardboard box, and I find a ceramic blade bank in the shape of a frog (blade banks were made to safely dispose of old razor blades) and the thing is priced at $65, which is twice what I'd sell it for, I get annoyed. My thought is that if the vendor doesn't respect his merchandise by presenting it in a neat and orderly fashion, why should I? If I walked into Tiffany's and had to forage through a box-lot of diamond necklaces to find one I liked, I don't think I'd want to pay $12,000 for the thing.

CONTIGUITY: Simply put, the value of an item increases when it is surrounded by valuable items. Conversely, its value diminishes when surrounded by garbage. To re-enter Tiffany's for a moment, you will not find a box-lot of diamond necklaces, but rather find that necklace you love surrounded by a dozen other beautiful necklaces, and hundreds of other exquisitely crafted rings, bracelets, earrings and watches. Contiguity of beautiful pieces contributes to expectation, which we discussed above. Take that same diamond necklace and place it in the middle of a rhinestone display, on the table of a dealer who specializes in costume jewelry, and put the same $12,000 price tag on it, and you would have a hard time selling it to anyone who isn't a diamond expert. (And he'll ask to buy it for six!) When you get a reputation for quality, and display only quality items, each piece will help every other piece.

CRITICAL MASS: This is an interesting psychological phenomenon, having to do with perception. Put one nice Limoge egg cup on your table and you will likely have difficulty selling it at the price you think it is worth. Put a dozen different Limoge egg cups on your table and people will stop to "ooh" and "ah." It might be that they simply don't see the single item. The eye travels over it; it doesn't impress the mind. And if they do see it, somehow they discount it. But the collection does impress—there's strength in numbers. And by having a number of different items in the same category grouped together, all attractive and in good condition, you will create a critical mass that makes it easier to sell any one of them.

Human Environment

The human environment describes all the personal ways in which people, both sellers and buyers, interact with objects.

THE SELLER: You walk up to a table and see a collection of feature matches that are just beautiful. Feature matches are the ones that have a picture printed on the matchsticks themselves. They were giveaways of the early to middle Twentieth Century, and advertised restaurants and clothing chains, individual products, everything. As you used the matches, you destroyed the image, so here we have one of the few collectibles that literally went up in smoke. You think it would be neat to start a small collection of feature matches, and you begin to ask the dealer some questions. Unbeknownst to you, the dealer has an array of personal issues that will directly affect this transaction. Did he have health problems last year that prevented him from selling for six months, and cost half his life savings? If he did, it could significantly affect his business model; he may need cash, and therefore lower prices on all his merchandise including your matches. Conversely, he may have had a healthy, prosperous year and feel flush; he might actually be a net buyer this year, purchasing more collectibles than he sells, expanding his personal collections, and more interested in showing off his lovely feature matches than selling them. How much inventory does the seller have? Did he recently buy a thousand feature matchbooks, and feel the need to relieve himself of some of that inventory, and get a piece of his investment back? How well have feature matches been selling over the last year or two? He may love them, but if he finds that they don't sell, his price will come down. How much space does he have in his apartment or house? How old is he? At some point, a dealer has to call it quits, and a general liquidation of inventory occurs.

THE BUYER: Similar questions pertain to the buyer. Who is the buyer? Is he a picker, a dealer, a collector, an investor? Pickers, who have a limited outlet for resale, will pay less than dealers, and dealers, who must make a profit, will pay less than collectors. People who buy to invest are wild cards. Since they are buying for the wrong reason, they can make expensive mistakes.

But there are also more general aspects to the human environment.

CATEGORY: The category represented by the item is a factor in determining price, because more people are attracted to some categories than to others. An advertising trade card that promotes a tobacco company is more desirable than one that promotes a type of barbed wire because there are more collectors of tobacco items than people who collect different examples of barbed wire. And yes, there are a small number of fanatics who collect barbed wire, and other types of fencing, used in settling the west. It is hard to think of any category that *doesn't* have its collectors. An auction of tobacco items will bring out more bidders, and that will lead to generally higher prices. But this does not mean that a single piece of extremely rare barbed wire won't sell for an unbelievable sum.

So the rule should be thought of in this way: That a popular category makes it *easier* to find a buyer for your collectible because there are more of them, and the larger number competing for your collectible has the general affect of keeping prices up. But – no surprise in this world of Post-Modernism and Chaos – exceptions to this rule abound.

There are not many collectors of old Levi® jeans. In fact, I would guess that even experienced dealers may not look twice at a pair of old jeans in a closet of a house they had bought (the contents of the house, that is, not the structure) and were cleaning out. I think, however, more people will pay attention to old Levi® jeans when they learn that a 19th Century pair was recently put up for auction on eBay®. The final bid was $15,000, and the jeans did not sell because the seller's reserve price was not met!

And last, to show that even experienced dealers some-times have their minds boggled: At Brimfield, recently, the dealer one tent over was displaying a ball of string. This ball was about two feet in diameter. Now, I have been in this business for fifteen years, and never saw anyone try to sell a ball of string. Well, my neighbor displayed it, talked about it, and sold it. For $500. Apparently, a larger one had sold recently at one of the premier auction houses for a couple of thousand. I tip my hat to my colleague, and I think I tip my hat to the buyer, too, but I'm not sure. $500. For a ball of string. I know it took years to collect and wind, and it is certainly a piece of Americana. But still. A ball of string! You gotta love this business.

Also, if an item crosses categories, it will add potential buyers. As an example, a poster of Joe Lewis endorsing Wendell Willkie for President will appeal to three sets of collectors: Those who collect posters, those who collect sports figures (particularly those who collect boxing) and those who collect political items. At auction, the price will rise as each set of collectors, in effect, bids against the others.

HOT CATEGORIES AND FADS: For reasons that seem to have more to do with chaos theory than psychology, some categories inexplicably become hot. Fountain pens became hot in the early 90s. The interest lasted a few years, then an ice age descended. I look today at price guides from the mid-90s, and I see pens that were priced at $250 then, fetching $30 on eBay® now. Baseball cards went through a nova of their own. When mania hits a category that was never a collectible before, we call it a fad, and sensible advice is to stay away from all things that are suddenly and inexplicably valued. Remember Cabbage Patch® dolls? We recently passed through the throes of a Beanie Babies® craze. The value of a collectible does not necessarily go straight up, a lesson we learned when looking at how generations collect objects from their own childhood.

Items acquire value over time, but they can lose value, too. Buying the latest fad falls into the "Greater Fool" business model. Yes, you say, it may be foolish to buy a Beanie Baby® for $100, but you are sure you can sell it for $150. Maybe so. But it is a game of musical chairs, and when the music stops many of us will be left with very expensive Pet Rocks in our dresser drawer.

A word on irrationality and emotion in antiques and collectibles: The question arises as to why there is a herd mentality in this business, as well as in so many other areas of life. In the early 1600s, the tulip bulb was introduced into Holland, which was a prosperous country at the time. This bulb, beautiful and rare, became a status symbol for the rich and powerful. Its popularity soared, demand skyrocketed, and in 1636 traders began speculating. Prices for single bulbs reached the levels of prices for contemporary houses. Finally, a year later, a single lot of rare bulbs did not sell. Panic ensued, the bubble burst, prices returned to sane levels, and recently won fortunes were lost. But that was nearly 400 years ago. It couldn't happen today. Not in collectibles. Not in the stock market. We're smarter today, aren't we?

Clearly, it is difficult to stand on the sidelines when the bandwagon is rolling down the street. If everyone began to value tulip bulbs, I would be an idiot not to take the opportunity to sell any I might own into that emerging bull market. Nor is it irrational for me to recognize the mania for what it is, and buy and sell quickly for short-term gain (even though it contributes to the hysteria, and helps the herd grow). The obvious irrationality begins when you come to believe that an historic paradigm has been breached – that tulip bulbs (or tech stocks) now deserve their huge value, that that value will continue to climb, and that that value is secure.

But there is another piece of irrationality that is a characteristic of groups, one less obvious, and which as individuals within groups we cannot easily avoid. The fact is that groups as a whole act in ways far less intelligently, far less maturely, and far more emotionally than do any of the single individuals within the group. For at least a century, psychologists have noted this, and written about "group madness," or "group contagion." Gustave Le Bon wrote about the madness of the mob during the French Revolution, when the guillotine fell on guilty and innocent alike. Wilfred Bion, a British psychiatrist, described the necessity for a "binocular vision," (in group life, the ability to see the contributions of both individuals and of the group-as-a-whole) in his work with convalescent soldiers in the 1940s. In our own history, how do we explain lynch mobs that arose out of ordinary citizens, who, individually, would be incapable of such murderous acts? Nor do we need such drama or examples distant in time and place. We need only let our minds wander to the last time we served on a committee. A job that one or two people might handle quite well becomes a mire when eight or twelve attack it. I don't need to go into the theory, which is detailed and draws on psychoanalytic principles. But for me, this idea of emotional regression in groups goes a long way to explaining why, at an auction, reason often leaves me, my desire for the object increases as the price rises, and my hand shoots up with a will of its own.

Interestingly, one does not have to be in a physical crowd to feel the tug of the group. Alone in my office, scanning the multitude of items for sale on eBay® (too many to give conscious thought to all) I find my attention drawn to the ones which have already received bids. Why? Because if these items have bids, they must have merit, right? Other buyers think so. Items neglected probably deserve to be neglected; that is my unexpressed and largely unnoticed thought.

We are all part of the herd.

PERSONAL VALUES: Everyone is different, and our individual psychologies affect what we buy and how we sell. It regularly happens that I make a buying mistake. I overpay, or there is a flaw in the item I didn't notice. When I do this, my inclination is to sell the thing quickly, so I don't have to look at it week after week and beat myself up for my stupidity. If I've overpaid, I'll try to get my money back, or even take a small loss. (My cousin Paul calls this paying Stupid Tax.) For me, it is worth sacrificing a few bucks to not have to keep dealing with my mistake.

Occasionally, I inherit stuff I would never buy. Paul has an aunt, Sonya, who recently died. I helped Paul, and his wife, Avery, clean out Sonya's apartment. I was invited to take what I could use; everything else would be thrown out. (More of this story later.) At the end, Avery insisted that I take Sonya's old coats, which were in excellent condition and dated from the 1950s. I took an armful, and eventually brought them to Brimfield and hung them on a fence. Sure enough, I had inquiries, and I made up prices. $60 for this fake leopard. No? Okay, $50. No? How about $45? I sold them at $45, at $40, at $30, and the last one at $22. The point is, by the end of that week I had sold all the coats! I did that because they cost me nothing, and because I didn't really care about them, and I would accept whatever the market brought.

There were two lessons here for me. Like other vendors, I sometimes fall in love with my merchandise. I decide what the value *should* be, and when the market disagrees, I stubbornly insist that the market is wrong. (Lesson: Unless I love something so much that I'm willing to take it out of my inventory and put it on my own display shelf, I have to admit that the market is more right than I am, and I try to adjust the price accordingly.) Again, like most vendors I do not want to take a loss. Even when I've made a buying mistake, I keep looking for that one customer who will bale me out. I have a basement full of stuff looking for that one customer who is never going to appear. (Expanded Lesson: You will sometimes have to adjust your price and take a loss. Do it! In baseball, a .300 hitter is doing very well. You should do better than that, but you will not make money on everything you buy.)

As the alert reader has noticed, everything I say has an exception. It also happens that nearly every time I set up at a market, I sell something I have had for years, in which no one in memory has shown any interest. So it is true that in the fullness of time everything will sell, and at your price. It becomes, finally, an individual decision: How long will you hold onto an item, live with it, pack it and unpack it? For myself, life is short. I prefer quick turnovers, even for less money.

I have specific personal preferences, too, for what I choose to buy. If I see an oak table for a $100, and I know I can easily get $300 for it, I still won't buy it. The thing weighs more than I do. I would have to take it apart to fit it into my car. I know I would strain my back lugging it around. I created a shopping rule a long time ago: "There are some profits not worth taking." I repeat that mantra, again and again when I am walking the fields. As a rule, I will not buy items that are too bulky, too heavy, or too breakable. As a rule, I will not buy items that need fixing up, and I also am reluctant to buy items that are plain, inconspicuous, or ugly. I want small things, light things. Metal is nice because it is hard to break. I want inventory that, in real estate lingo, has "curb appeal." I want people drawn to my tables by something visually interesting or exciting. If they don't come over and look, they won't buy.

Note: As a rule, I only sometimes follow my rules.

A final word on how the Human Environment affects the value of collectibles. Worth is also a function of how much work and time you put into selling your item. If you take the time to learn about it, if you consult guide books and auction results, if you make the effort (and sometimes incur the expense) to find the right buyer, the item will sell well.

About price guides and auction results: Beware! They often have little correlation with the prices you will get at a flea market or at a show, and, if they do, that usefulness will be short lived. Regionality will distort values published in price guides, and condition is usually not well explained. Likewise, auction results provide a clue as to what the item is worth, but that auction was a particular event. At least two people wanted the thing (unless you were there, you don't know for sure that there were more bidders) and only one of them was willing to pay the realized price. Remember, the underbidder was not! That collectible is now gone. If you have another, exactly the same on your shelf, and it goes on the block tomorrow, all we know is

ONE person will be interested, and if a competitor does not emerge the price will be drastically less. Price guides and realized auction prices are useful as indicators only, and will give you ballpark figures for your collectibles, but nothing more. In this matter eBay® is an excellent source for checking current realized prices on specific collectibles.

eBay® and Technology

In one decade – the 1990s – the internet arrived, eBay®
opened its cyber-doors, and nothing about buying and
selling collectibles has been the same. Some of us came to
the party early, some later. A few of us, the curmudgeon
crowd that never gave up its typewriters, are still computer illiterate. But dinosaurs die. None of us doubts the fact
that email and the internet will change communication and
marketing the way the telephone did a hundred years ago.

At first, eBay® seemed a novelty. A world-wide public
auction? Through telephone wires? Costing only a few
pennies? Where anyone who had a computer and a modem
could bid on my Steiff® Teddy Bear? What a thought! Even
without pictures (at the beginning, digital cameras were
far too expensive) even without high-speed access, it was
an astonishing business model. In less time than it took to
boot up, *everyone* in the collectibles business was talking
about eBay®; two years later everyone was doing it.

Consider the advantages.

No longer did we have to awake in the dark, load our
vans, set up in the cold and suffer the wind and rain and
frost and heat to sell our wares. No longer did we have to
pay rent for space, carry our yogurts and sandwiches in
coolers, and try to find a decent cup of coffee. No longer
did we have to leave our valuables unattended as we quickly and nervously found a Port-O-Potty. Now we could sit
comfortably in our warm houses, sip hot coffee, and take
our bathroom breaks in ease and comfort as, for less than
a buck, we could post our Baccarat Crystal Decanter for the
world to see. Our items would be up for auction from three
to ten days, and when it was over and a winning bidder
declared, we would only have to sit back and collect the
checks. What luxury! Who would ever go to a flea market
again?

Well, lots of us. But let us stay with eBay® for the moment, and describe, for those who live under a rock, what selling on this internet auction site is like.

There is the business of starting up – the computer to buy and master, the camera to purchase and learn, and the expense of a high speed internet connection, a must unless you really enjoy watching grass grow.

Then there is dealing with eBay® itself – opening an account, and giving them your credit card number so they can conveniently bill you for their commissions each month. Now, eBay® is not the only auction site. But it was the first, and it is the biggest. It has the "eyes." Hundreds of thousands of people click on every day. There may be competition in the future, but at the moment eBay® is *the* internet auction site, and serious buyers and sellers rarely look elsewhere.

And last but certainly not least, are all the steps that begin with listing your item and end with taking your check or money order to the bank and posting feedback. Feedback is a public forum for buyers and sellers to either praise or complain about the party on the other side of the transaction. For the uninitiated, it goes something like this.

eBay® Procedure

BUY THE ITEM. This is not a trivial statement. As you go along, you will find that certain collectibles sell well on eBay®, while others do not. And you will begin to shop with an eye for those sellable items. It goes without saying that top of the line merchandise will command the best price in cyberspace just as it will in the touch-world. But the exceptional aspect of eBay® is that in one week you can bring a greater number of interested eyes to your item than at any dozen shows, and it is these potential buyers with a *specific* interest in your category that make some items perfect eBay® auction pieces.

As you look at an item, considering whether or not to buy it for sale on eBay®, ask yourself a few questions. Is the piece common or is it unique? Does it have a specific local interest? Who do you think is going to bid and why? The perfect eBay® item is unusual or rare in an acceptable category and needs to reach a specific (if small) audience of collectors. Here's one example. I recently bought a CDV (Carte de Visite, an old photograph) of a 19th Century Turkish Sultan. I bought it from an experienced dealer who sets up in the middle of Manhattan, and he sold it to me for $5. He believed he could not have gotten much more for it. What were the chances, he thought, that someone would come by looking for photographs of early Turkish rulers willing to pay $15 or $20 for one? I bought it, put it on eBay®, and found an audience of several people from around the world who wanted it. The 7-day auction closed at $32. Here was an item that a limited number of people might want, and which was hard to publicize. eBay® did the work for me.

Here is another example. For years, I had an old dog license issued in Vermont in 1884 in my 3-ring binder filled with ephemera. It had been one item in a carton of paper I bought years ago, and I'd already recouped my investment in the "lot." So I had it priced at $12, and would have willingly come down to $10 if someone was interested. Either no one saw it, or no one liked it because the small square of paper just sat. I recently took a picture and put it up for auction on eBay®. I listed it under the category of Paper/Ephemera, and after one week of bidding it closed at $22.50. The result is no mystery. My dog license was no longer hidden in a 3-ring binder, but posted in an auction that attracted thousands of eyes every day. More important, it attracted the eyes of people who were interested in that highly specific category. I put the words "Dog license" in the title as well as the word "Vermont." Anyone who did a search through eBay® for "dog" or "license" or "Vermont" would have my license appear on their screen. In one week, I found four people who wanted it, which was all I needed. How else could I have found those four interested buyers? So, looking back, I see that this was a perfect eBay® item. And knowing that, I can see that I also own many terrible eBay® items. I have hundreds of relatively common political pinback buttons. These will sell at a flea market for anywhere from $1 to $5 each. They won't sell at all on eBay®. Not even for $1. They are too common. For example, I have a few dozen pins that say "Nixon Now." I put these pins out at the flea market for $1 each, and someone comes along and thinks it would be fun to wear that 1972 pin during the upcoming election, just as a gag. He gives me a dollar, puts on the pin, and laughs happily over his cheap impulse buy. Would that man bid on that "Nixon Now" pin on eBay® for $1? First of all, it wouldn't be $1. It would be $1 plus shipping, which would double the cost or more. Then he would have to spend a minute entering his bid. Then he'd have to spend another few minutes emailing me, confirming that he won the pin, and providing me with his address. Then he'd have to spend 4 or 5 minutes writing out a check, addressing the envelope for the check (increasing his cost by paying for postage) and mailing the check. And then he'd have to wait ten days to get the thing. For a common "Nixon Now" pin? No way!

As you walk the markets, you will begin to learn what is common in a category. This is important knowledge. When you see something you haven't seen before, buy it! This is what sells, both on eBay®, as well as at markets and shows.

TAKE A GOOD SCAN OR PHOTO. I am amazed at how many bad photos I see on eBay® – too distant to show detail, or out of focus, or taken on a kitchen table alongside a half dozen distracting items. Spend some time with your photo, shooting and editing it. In the case of eBay®, your picture *is* worth a thousand words. Once your photo is saved in your computer, eBay® lets you transfer it directly to the auction page. As I write this, your first photo is free and each additional one is 15¢– a good service, reasonably priced.

Now you must **LIST YOUR ITEM IN AN APPROPRIATE CATEGORY**, or double list it for an additional fee. Category and title are extremely important. Most collectors and dealers do title searches in specific categories. Make sure all key words are in the title, so people who may have a specific interest in your item will actually find it.

Find **SECURE STORAGE** in your home for your listed items. For small collectibles, a drawer dedicated to this purpose is good enough. There is nothing worse than misplacing an item you have put up for auction.

ANSWER EMAIL QUESTIONS, if any arise. eBay® provides bidders and potential bidders with the seller's email address. This communication during the auction period is important. Many times, as a buyer, I have needed information about an item, which was not in the picture or description. When an answer came back, in a timely fashion, I felt comfortable about bidding. There is no getting around it: Responsible and accurate communication increases sales.

After the auction is over, **EMAIL THE BUYER** informing him that he has won the item, give the final bid price and any costs for shipping or insurance, and include your address.

When the winning bidder responds to your email, **RECORD THAT HE HAS RESPONDED**. Buy shipping supplies in bulk if you can. This makes life easier, gives you a professional look, and limits shipping costs. I keep a generous supply of padded envelopes and boxes of various sizes. I also bought a roll of self-stick labels, with my home address pre-printed. These are a little expensive, but very convenient. I write out the label the moment the winning bidder has emailed me his address. Then when the check arrives, the label is ready and the package is quickly assembled for shipping. If the buyer doesn't respond to your email notification after a week or so, and if a check hasn't arrived, send a nice "reminder" email note and record that you've done so. Occasionally, the bidder will walk away from the transaction. He will not reply to emails, and you will not hear from him again. After a few weeks of attempting to reach him, you can find, on the auction page, the underbidder (the person who came in second in the auction) and offer the item to that bidder at his slightly lower price. Or you can re-list it.

As a rule, if your item does not sell, I would not suggest that you re-list it immediately. It is tainted goods, at least for the moment. Wait a few months and re-list it then. However, new bidders enter the eBay® market every week. Your item will be new for them. Recently, in the course of one month, two of my items did not sell. One (a collection of LBJ campaign pins) was priced to start at $9.95, the other (two Adlai Stevenson pins) at $6. I re-listed them both immediately. The LBJ collection ended up selling for $20; Adlai went for $14 and change. In both cases the winning bidders had low feedback numbers, which meant they were newcomers to eBay®.

When you receive the check or money order in the mail, **RECORD THAT PAYMENT HAS BEEN RECEIVED**, and enter the date the item will be shipped.

SHIP THE ITEM. I know I am in the minority, but I ship winning bids the day after the check has arrived. If the winning bidder wants to send a money order, that's fine, but I don't insist on it. Purchasing a money order is inconvenient, and becomes another expense. I am pleased to save my customers that small fee, and I tell them I ship the next day regardless of the form of payment. My items are low-end, the checks I receive are generally under $50, and I haven't yet had one bounce. (Yes, I would not be so easy about it all if I sold something for $500. If someone sent me a check for that amount, I would probably wait a week to be certain it clears.) If you are hesitant about shipping quickly, click onto the feedback file of the buyer. A high, positive rating means that this is an experienced eBay®

customer, and you are unlikely to have trouble. Shipping immediately means fewer chances that the item will be forgotten or lost, and it is much appreciated by the customer. I also ship internationally. If a foreign bidder wins my item, I go to the Post Office and learn how much the packet will cost and I charge the bidder accordingly. I have opened PayPal and BidPay accounts, and I would probably use them regularly if I began to sell expensive items.

Note: PayPal and BidPay are two electronic payment services. At this moment, PayPal is free to the buyer, and the seller is charged a small fixed fee as well as a percent of the sale; BidPay is free to the seller, and the buyer is charged a fixed fee. If one is doing a lot of eBay® business, these services guarantee the funds and provide good value. With PayPal, transfer is instantaneous. You may ask them to mail you a check for the monies received into your account (there is a small charge for this service), but you can also leave your money in the account to pay for auctions you won. These payment services are most convenient for international purchases, since they also easily and accurately convert currencies.

POST POSITIVE FEEDBACK if the transaction went well. The "Feedback" file is a nice eBay® touch. Every time you buy or sell something, you are permitted to post your comments in the other party's feedback file, which is open for all to see. These comments can be positive or negative. In the case of someone walking away from an auction, it is appropriate to leave negative feedback so that other buyers and sellers are warned.

A Word on eBay®
Buyers Honor All Bids!

When the auction is over, contact the seller by email immediately. He wants to know you are there.

Write your check, send your money order, or arrange for electronic payment as soon as the seller informs you of the total price. (Even if you think you have overbid, and are now experiencing buyer's remorse!) Procrastination is more than just a thief of time, it is poor manners and bad business.

Some people send cash through the mail. No sane person advises this, but at the same time I've never had an envelope containing cash lost. People like to complain about the Postal Service, but they really do a remarkable job.

Buying on eBay® requires discipline. It is a lot easier to impulsively click your mouse than it is to drag your tired bottom off the couch, put on a coat, brave the February cold, and check out a collectibles show three towns away. Try to exercise restraint. If you are a dealer, it is best to buy for specific customers; if you are a collector, buy for your particular collection wants. Unless you are very rich, try not to buy just because the price seems low.

If you write a check or send a money order, be sure to include a description of the item you have purchased. Many dealers have a dozen or more auctions running continuously. A check without a description (or the eBay® number of the item) is hard for the seller to trace.

If the item arrives and it is not as described or pictured, contact the seller. Most will honor any complaint with a refund (usually minus shipping charges). I feel that my reputation (and my feedback file) are more important than any one sale, and most sellers would agree with me.

E-Tips

Keep customers' names and e-ddresses. Build a base of private clients who you can sell to directly.

Don't glut the market. It sometimes happens that I buy an item in quantity. It might be a very fine item. I recently bought 10 handsome pinback buttons featuring a picture of Secretariat, and issued as a memorial to that great horse winning the Belmont Stakes. I bought them for $1 each. I put one up on eBay® and it sold for $7. The next sold for $5. I waited a few months and listed a third; it fetched $23. There is no telling what an eBay® item will bring. Generally, I find the following 10/5/1 rule to hold: Of any ten items I put up for auction, five will not sell at all. Of the five that sell, four will fetch less than what I would have wanted to get at a flea market or show. The last will sell for a number higher than I could ever imagine. Trouble is, I never know which will be the rocket, and which will be the duds. eBay® is a business of averages. But I do know enough not to flood my own market. I will wait several months more before I put up my fourth Secretariat pin.

As I reflect, it seems to me that the four items that sold for disappointing sums, averaged about 75% of what I considered acceptable retail prices. This is an interesting number because it is slightly too low a price for the dealer to be happy with the sales, and at the same time slightly too high a price for another dealer to jump in and buy. It is a good price for the collector, who wants a particular item, but only if that item is indeed as represented in the description and the photo. However, it is also a fact of eBay® that about one of four items purchased is *not* exactly as represented (the discrepancy may be too small to warrant a return) and so the collector will give back much of that 25% over time. If this analysis holds, eBay® is a remarkably efficient market.

In the same vein, don't compete against yourself. Items that were part of the 1960s anti-Vietnam War movement (posters, documents, pinback buttons) are "hot" now and are commanding premium prices. (Note: That era is 30-40 years removed. The generation who lived through that decade is now in its prime collecting years.) I buy items from the Sixties whenever I can find them, and I have dozens in stock. But I only offer them on eBay® one at a time. I don't want two of my auctions competing against each other for collector dollars.

Timing is everything. I recently purchased, as part of a lot, a small Shirley Temple child's ring. The lot consisted of six Shirley Temple pieces; I paid $10 for all. I kept wanting to list the ring on eBay®, but each time I tried, I did a search and found at least two identical rings up for auction already. Over a few months, I followed four or five of those Shirley Temple rings, and saw that they sold for between $8 and $12 each. Finally, I drew a blank. No Shirley Temple ring on eBay®! Quickly, I listed mine. For some reason, and I don't know why, my ring closed at $32. (This was a "1" in the 10/5/1 rule.) It might be that there was something different about this ring that collectors noticed and that brought the high price. But I don't think so. I think I was a little attentive and a lot lucky.

Since eBay® takes its lowest commission for items that begin under $10, that's where I usually start the auction. I believe an item that ends up selling for $30 will get there whether you start it at $1 or at $5 or at $9.95. However, it may not get there if you start it at $25! The too high starting price may take away from the competitive aspect of the auction, and leave you with either one bidder at your price, or no bidders at all. The lower price gets more people involved, and when a group gets involved – well, you know how I feel about the irrationality of groups. The trick is to let it work for you as the seller, and try not to succumb to it as the buyer. The trick, as Kipling says, is to keep *your* head while others all about you are losing theirs.

Other eBay® Benefits

eBay® is labor intensive, but that might be a good thing. As a rule, the more you work at it, the more you will get paid. It teaches the virtue of "get rich slow"—a nice lesson for those of us who sky-rocketed and crashed in the go-go Eighties, who saw thousands of dollars an hour enter our stock portfolios in the Nasdaq Nineties, and then leave at an even faster pace.

At a low enough starting price, most everything sells. Even given the 10/5/1 rule. Even if you only get your money back on some things. Even if you take an occasional small loss. The stuff will be gone, and you will have cash in your pocket. For anyone with a buying habit worthy of a 12-step program, this is a blessing indeed.

Cost to buyer and seller is reduced to a minimum. eBay® takes a nominal posting fee, and a very small percent of the sale. Moreover, you don't have to travel to the shows. Sellers save show fees, and everyone saves on gas, tolls, and most importantly, time.

And, since eBay® brings the show to the people, it is a godsend for those who, through geography, illness, or choice lead isolated lives.

People in small towns and localities can find objects connected to their own histories. A year or so ago, I sold a pin that said, "Mechanicsburg, For the Loan." I had no idea where Mechanicsburg was or what Loan to which it referred, but I didn't have to know. People who lived there did, and a few of them wanted the pin. I had another pin that said, "Dowd for Mayor." I didn't know any Dowds, but there were Dowds out there, and, as it turned out, one of them was related to this Mayor Dowd and bought her ancestor's image. Who said technology can't warm a heart?

eBay® has changed the nature of business relationships. I have bought from and sold to hundreds of people I've never met, and probably never will meet. Sometimes our emails are brief exchanges of addresses and monies to be sent, but sometimes we exchange pleasantries as well, appreciation for the courtesy and professionalism of our transaction, even personal information. In a strange, 21st Century way, I feel I have gotten to know some of my cyber-customers, and nearly all of my transactions with them cheer my day. Just the other month, I won a James Bond pin for $3. I paid by PayPal, and the pin didn't come and didn't come and didn't come. I notified the seller, who sent back a most apologetic email. He told me he had shipped the pin, obviously it was lost, and he was going to refund my cost. I said let's wait. Although I do not like to criticize our Post Office, sometimes it does develop a knot, and things show up much later than they should. My new friend did not listen to me, but posted my refund on PayPal the next day. Sure enough, later that morning the pin arrived. I wrote the good news, he wrote back asking that I keep the pin and the refund, too, for my inconvenience. I wrote back saying, no! And I ended up winning our little Alphonse-Gaston routine by refusing his refund. I know we're only talking about $3, but here was an interaction that made both of us feel better than any $3 in our pockets ever could. I find courtesy and consideration frequently in eBay® transactions. The level of compliance is extraordinary. Cynics, take heed! Few people walk away from bids, and, knock on wood, I have not yet received a bad check. Correlative Point: In cyberspace, you are still your business. You need to pay attention to detail, and to communicate. You need to be fair. People must have faith in you, perhaps even more so than at flea markets and shows.

eBay® is educating the world. Auction results are listed for everyone to see. Anyone who cares can determine what is common in a certain category, and what is scarce. On this global bulletin board, it is impossible to argue that a Princess Diana commemorative plate is worth more than $20 when it regularly sells on eBay® for less.

This education is creating a trend away from regional disparities in pricing, and towards a global market. And this, in turn, will reduce the advantage that the collector and vendor who lives near a large city has had over his rural counterpart. A specialist of barbershop collectibles in Alaska can now compete with one living in Ohio. A Belgian can sell an eye cup to an American just as easily (and at twice the price) as he can sell it to another Belgian at a local market. We are truly heading for a democratic international pricing structure for collectibles.

Let me clarify a point as I dive into water well over my head. I am here not talking about "globalization", which advocates the free flow of capital across borders, and is used by multi-national corporations in ways that are anything but democratic. I am instead talking about a kind of global people's capitalism in which everyone can join, and which ultimately can provide a true market price for a commodity, in this case collectibles. eBay® and the internet instantly provide mass information. If that information is truthful (and in every market there is a chance of fraud) then the internet joins buyers around the world, who, even as they compete with each other, form a baffle against the sort of seller who wishes to protect his profit by controlling his sale.

As I view it, this democratic capitalism holds, as an ideal, a market that becomes more efficient and fair as it expands through technology. More information is spread to more people with a goal of everyone having equal access to information and markets. Armed with information, people will learn what is common and what is rare. Then, under the law of supply and demand, and without restrictions, the market will assure that truly rare items rise in price while truly common ones fall. And the middle will get narrower. Going back to the example at the start of this essay, when I know I can always find a Prince Albert tin for $3 on eBay®, I will not buy it for $6 from a dealer at a flea market. Furthermore, I may not buy one at *any* price because I know it is common and will always be there if I want it.

However, the above analysis is an ideal. A democratic capitalism may be your goal and mine, but historically it has not been the goal of capitalists who know their profits will fall in truly free markets. What else are tariffs and protectionism? Witness the legal problems of Sotheby's and Christie's chief executives pleading guilty to commission rate-fixing. Witness the legal problems of Microsoft®. The capitalist looks to control the market for his advantage – create short supply and eliminate competition. He has his rationale. He has made the investment, taken the risk, and done the work. He has earned his profit. But all too regularly a deserved profit turns to either unfairly stifling the opposition or gouging the public, which governments try to regulate with mixed results. It would be curious if the internet did the job naturally and effectively if left alone.

The Other Side of the E-Coin

We've looked at the obvious benefits that eBay® brings to the collectibles market. But eBay® does not have all the advantages; there are benefits to selling at flea markets, shows, and at real-life auctions, as well.

As the seller, you set the price of your merchandise at a show. And as a buyer, you get to see an asked price and negotiate down, not see a starting price and compete with other buyers to bid that price up.

At shows, you don't have the competition that surrounds you on eBay® where hundreds of items similar to yours are being offered for sale at that very same moment, and if your item is common there may be several of the *exact* item being offered.

eBay® is labor intensive compared to a show. In one hour, a dealer can put hundreds of items on his tables. On eBay® an item can take 10 minutes or more to "put out" to the public.

Many customers who come to flea markets and shows do not surf the net. They don't know they can get it for less on eBay®, and in many cases they don't care. Immediacy and convenience – seeing the item and being able to take it with them directly after buying it – are more important than saving a few dollars. For these people, a photo is not good enough. There is no depth in a picture. Colors are not the same. You don't get every angle even from a batch of pictures. These people live tactilely; they need to hold objects in their hands, to examine them slowly and carefully, to feel them emotionally as well as physically before they buy.

Since more and more show customers are also surfing the net, the question arises as to what effect eBay® will have on total vendor income. Given the volume of eBay® business, it only makes sense that the numbers of dollars spent at shows, flea markets, and antique stores will diminish. But for many vendors, this will not matter because they are sharing the eBay® pie. Assuming the U.S. economy stabilizes, and begins to grow again, between new eBay® sales and (even diminished) show or flea market sales, the total number of dollars taken in by dealers through the year is apt to stay the same, or even grow. There will be new dollars coming in from folks who live in upper Montana or west Texas and the like, who can't regularly get to shows. It is only that the stream of income will now be split between internet and live sales.

A prestigious show or auction provides an imprimatur. People want the Sotheby's stamp, the Christie's guarantee of authenticity. The provenance attached to items sold at such powerful venues adds to price. Real-world auctions can create a buzz that eBay® cannot duplicate. There is little time pressure on eBay® (except, of course, for the last minute of an auction when fingers fly over keyboards and swipers do their nasty work). You might have a week to decide the very top amount you wish to pay for that Egyptian scarab. But when people bid against each other, eye to eye, in a live auction that may last a total of ninety seconds, restraint is more difficult. Also, eBay® does not specifically advertise high-end merchandise. At a premier auction house your attention is directed, you are educated by the auctioneer, your guarantee of authenticity is absolute. You are surrounded by knowledgeable buyers who, by a show of hands, are telling you that the Sioux basket on the pedestal *is* worth the $2000 one of them just bid. You only have to decide if you want to go to $2100. In a nutshell, as a buyer at a reputable live auction you have guarantees that you don't get on eBay®. While as a seller, if you are fortunate enough to own a Picasso, you probably don't want to sell it on eBay®, even with the reduced commission.

The reverse of this is "caveat emptor," and items posted for sale on eBay® come with that disclaimer. No one authenticates them. Recently a daguerreotype was put up for auction. The owner claimed it was the first known photograph of Abraham Lincoln, and the starting price was $14 million. Under the photo was a statement by an expert in such matters who said he had compared this image with other known Lincoln images, and in his opinion, this was unquestionably an early photo of our 16th President. Problem was, to my eyes, and apparently to the eyes of others, the man pictured in the "dag" looked nothing like Abe. This is not to say he was or wasn't. It is only to say that my pebble on the beach is an arrowhead and that man is Lincoln only when two people agree. And it will be sold only when one of those two people is a buyer who, in this case, is $14 million worth convinced. One can only wonder why this historic portrait didn't end up at Sotheby's.

Finally, ultimately, we are active, social creatures. Some of us have strong aversions to groups and crowds, but in the main we feel a rush of adrenaline walking into a busy market. It just pleases the senses. So many people to look at, so many objects to see. The hum of business in our ears, a warming sun, food vendors with enticing aromas. Our imaginations fire with the hope of finding a treasure sitting on a table just beyond our vision. eBay® indeed has its virtues, but we are a social species. Television did not kill the movies, as many feared and a few predicted. Flea markets and antique shows will endure.

Epilogue

Sonya's apartment was in a section of Brooklyn that was squat and ugly, a place no one came to for pleasure. In the dark, cluttered living room, two Jamaican women sat on a sofa next to boxes of bric-a-brac. They had come to pay respects and to take a few mementos. My cousin, Paul, was talking to a man who made a business of buying pianos, and was now refusing Sonya's baby grand, even for free. Paul's wife, Avery, was by the window sorting photos. They had invited me to come along to see if there was anything I wanted to take for my flea market business before everything was thrown out.

Sonya was a family character – a small woman with a bundle of nervous energy that showed in a piercing voice and a facial tic. She lived alone, strident and arrogant—a hard woman to like. A "know-it-all," who accepted the scorn that comes with that role, because she did—she was right and the world was wrong. And on no subject was she more certain and furiously right than Israel.

Through the years, my aunt Milly defended her sister. "Sonny had a hard life," Mildred would tell us. "She's really very smart, and was quite a beauty in her day." Not easy for the younger generation to see, but Milly's defense of her sister was admirable even if it came from equal parts of love and guilt. Milly, after all, had everything Sonya did not have – a husband, who generously took care of his sister-in-law through her invalid years; a child; grandchildren; and a disposition that was as soft and accommodating as Sonny's was obdurate.

I remember when Sonya got married. It was in 1954; she was approaching forty and miraculously had found a man. His name was Arthur. He taught college and was a philosopher. I was impressed, because he told us he had corresponded with John Dewey. Arthur fit the philosopher cliché – mild and thoughtful. I liked him a lot and wondered why he had married Sonya. A few years later, Arthur had a heart attack and went into a hospital. When he came out he packed his bags and left.

It was creepy walking through the apartment. I felt like a vulture poking through the remains of this life. But then I always thought that vultures got a bad rap. They were not predators; they never ran down a prey and sunk sharp talons or incisors into a terrified animal smaller than themselves. They were peaceful birds, and useful – models of ecological virtue as they cleaned the landscape of carrion.

No help. It still felt creepy. But someone had to go through Sonya's dresser feeling for perhaps a packet of jewelry at the back of a drawer. If true valuables were found, they should not be thrown out. They should go to Milly, or Paul, or Paul's children. Surely Sonny would have wanted that.

But there were none. I found nothing that I would buy at a flea market for even loose change. Nevertheless, free is free, and I made a carton of a glass pitcher, some Israeli ashtrays, a pressed glass bowl, a deck of airline playing cards, a box of costume jewelry. Avery insisted that I take some of Sonya's coats, wonderful reminders of 1960s fashion and in perfect condition. Laura Petrie could have worn any one of them for an evening out with Rob. Feeling not guilty, but more and more depressed, I went through Sonny's desk and the closet behind it. Every paper of her life was there. Paul gave me some large black plastic bags, and I began filling them with the pounds of legal work that had consumed her life.

You see, Sonny had to sue. She had worked as a school administrator for the Board of Education of New York City. She was smart, probably did a good job, and earned a decent salary. But accidents and indignities constantly befell her, and she had to sue. Once she slipped on peas in the school cafeteria and wrenched her back. Another time she was on a subway which stopped abruptly, and she was thrown against a door and hurt her wrist. I think the City always paid her something to make her go away. Apparently she never did for long.

When I finished with the legal papers, I came to bills, then cards and letters. I read through some. Should I have not? I would certainly never have dreamt of doing this if she were alive. But I wouldn't be in this apartment if she were alive. I hadn't seen her in over 30 years! Still, it was hard to throw away those papers – the last of Sonya really – but Paul helped, and we did. At the end, I saw some envelopes with letters inside; they dated from the 1940s and had Palestine stamps. On impulse, I threw that handful into my carton; the stamps might be worth something.

I tried to parse my feelings as I drove home. There was nothing wrong with what I had done today. In fact, I was a help to my cousin. Still, it felt bad. Sonya's life was being trashed, literally, and I had taken some of it for personal gain. I would have felt less badly if I had liked Sonya, if my family and I hadn't turned her into a joke for 50 years. I would have felt less badly if I took her things because she meant something to me. For a moment, I envied the two Jamaican women who genuinely cared for Sonya.

A few days later, I noticed the packet of letters I had taken. I had a stamp price guide, and quickly determined that the Palestine stamps were of little value. Then I looked more carefully at the first envelope; it was dated April 25,

1944, and it was addressed to Sonya through the Jewish National Fund in Jerusalem. It was also hand stamped Army Post Office, and bore a sticker, which assured it had been examined by censors. With small butterflies in my stomach – please, someone, tell me why this was wrong to do – I opened the envelope and two letters fell out.

I read the first.

Dear Sonya,

Please forgive my lengthy abstinence from writing. I got your letter about 6 weeks ago and was hoping to spend a few days leave in Jerusalem shortly afterwards, but the curfew descended on Palestine like a blight, and wrecked my hopes.

I was distressed to hear that you had been ill and hope very much that the rest put you right, as you said it had, and that your boss has persuaded you to work a little less hard. The recent activities of the Stern Gang must have upset you considerably, and it is entirely damnable to think of the work that you and others are doing being over-clouded by the criminal gambits of a handful of lunatics.

But to return from the unpleasant general to the charming particular and talk about you again: have you had your holiday yet, or is it still to come, or aren't you going to have one this year? ... Have you been leading a quiet and decorous existence, or dancing and indulging in Camel Hock? This is indeed a crude barrage of interrogation, but it has the merit at least of making it plain that I should be happy to get a letter from you.

I've no news. Except that I've grown an idler, more cynical, and ever more unpleasant character than before, so, Sonya: You have been warned.

With love,

Robin

P.S.: How's the local bacon situation?

Sonny had a beau! Towards the end of World War II, living and working in Palestine, Sonya had met a young English officer named Robin Bury. There were certainly letters missing in the cache, because the second letter was dated Friday, Sept 8th.

Dear Robin,

On the theory that two hastily penned notes do not a letter make, I started another on Sunday (3rd) but decided to wait until my leave was approved.

Your letter brought me nearer to you than I have felt for a very long time. A retentive memory intervenes, however, and the more I think of your "leave" the worse I feel...

This week has been a very full one, what with straightening out the leave roster so I could get away as quickly as possible, arranging accommodation at Naharia by phone – and getting my leave approved. I shall be leaving Jerusalem Sunday, the 17th, shortly after noon and hope to reach Naharia by 6 at the latest. Meanwhile, if you want to get a message to me, I have already arranged with Tuffy to hold any mail for me. If you can telephone they will take the message.

Apropos the Japs, I quite agree that Britain and America must see it through together, but I fervently hope your gaze remains "myopic." You are already so much "that elusive Pimpernel" and the chances of your going farther afield before this phase of the war is over, so great, I wonder whether it will be a case of, "Bury – charming fellow – wonder where he is now and where if ever we shall meet again?" The rapid approach of the end of the war gives rise to a chain of personal reflection.

Wouldn't it be marvelous if the war ended when I got to Naharia and you were coming in to see me??

Am still hoping that no letter means you may come to Jerusalem before I leave. Tho' I could do with a letter as well.

Love,
Sonya

141

I picked up another envelope and read the letter quickly. It was written in Sonya's precise hand, and dated Sunday, October 29, 1944.

Robin darling,

Your belated letter of 27th Sept. arrived only a few days ago.

Have you ever really tried hard to make a train and arrived too late – and felt foolish? I did. After all my difficulty in getting away from the office, leaving for Naharia with an abscessed throat I contracted at the last moment, I felt wretched when I reached that "haven" and there was no word from you...

Dusty did what he could to allay my wounded feelings – took me to dinner with some of his friends. By the way, did you ever receive the hat he sent you? I believe it was in exchange for the hat you wore at the races! He also told me of that beautiful Arab Demoiselle at Kuman.

Returned to Jerusalem on the 4th October and still there was no word. It made me no happier to hear from Dusty just before I left Naharia that someone in the village had already received a letter from a chap in your unit, and that it took 15 days to arrive! Did you receive mine of 8th September, before you left here, and if not, has it caught up with you yet?

I've been scanning the newsreels closely. I haven't caught a glimpse of you so far. So will you please send me a photo to refresh my memory – if you haven't one of yourself alone, a group photo will do.

I am enclosing a snapshot of myself taken in a weak moment. Please forgive the scanty attire – it was taken at the beach... It is now 12:55 A.M. Goodnight, keep well, and do write more often. My love to you,

Sonya

Sonya young. Sonya flirtatious. "Please excuse the scanty attire," indeed! Sonya writing breezily with care and flair, letters just like ones I keep in the back of my filing cabinet from girls who are grandmothers now, but for whom once I longed.

I carefully returned this letter to its envelope, and now noticed all the handwriting and military stamps. I looked more closely. Under the Palestine Stamps, under the address to R.C.L. Bury, Special Boat Service, across from a stamp that said "Deputy Chief Field Censor" was another purple stamp that read, "Undelivered for Reason Stated, Return to Sender." And just below that, in a small tight hand, "Killed in Action, O2E for Disposal, CMF, 15/11/44." And on the back yet another stamp, "GHQ 2nd Echelon BNAF – Certified Deceased."

Sonya old, Sonya strident, Sonya fiercely defensive, blinking furiously while suing New York City.

I was grateful to feel the tears well up. This by-the-by flea market business had given me an unexpected gift. It had restored a member of my family. And it taught me what I always knew, but never in such a poignant way – that age is not easy and that all of us have our reasons. That we were all young once, and beautiful, and in love. And that the objects of our lives still hold the meanings of our journeys, and enrich those who follow.

About the Author

Barry Berg has received advanced degrees from the Yale School of Drama and the Environmental Psychology Program at the Graduate Center, CUNY. In addition, he has earned a Certificate from the William Alanson White Psychoanalytic Institute's program in Organizational Consultation and Development.

He has written plays, novels, and television while maintaining parallel careers as a consultant to small businesses and organizations and teaching Speech and Communication at the Borough of Manhattan Community College for twenty years. In the late 1980s, Mr. Berg began his own weekend business of buying and selling collectibles.

Today, Mr. Berg lives with his wife Susan and their son Julian in Maplewood, New Jersey, where he continues his writing, his consulting, and his collectibles business, and, in the past year, teaching Special Education in the local primary schools.